Know-How

Experience, Expertise and Execution

Edited by
Gail Rafter Meneley and Dev Mukherjee

ISBN: 000-0-0000-0000-0 *(sc)*
ISBN: 978-1-5142-2284-3 *(e)*

This book was printed in the United States of America.

For more information about Shields Meneley Partners contact:

Gail R. Meneley, Co-Founder and Principal
Shields Meneley Partners
311 South Wacker Drive - Suite 4550
Chicago, Illinois 60606

Chicago Direct: 312.994.9502
Lake Forest Direct: 847.295.4103

www.shieldsmeneley.com

Contents

Section 2: Creating the Most Value

Section 3: Unleashing Potential

Dedication

This book is dedicated to Donald S. Perkins, a dear friend, and member of the Shields Meneley Partners Advisory Board. On every Board there is one person to whom everyone turns for the final word based on their confidence in that person's wisdom, experience, and integrity. This was Don's role on our board and dozens of others he served over his 60 year career. He was warm and genuine, and mentored hundreds and hundreds of people from students to business and political leaders around the world. He died on March 25, 2015. The world will be a different place without him.

Foreword

Don Perkins

After more than 60 years in business – the first 20 as an operating leader and CEO and the last 40 on boards of directors of organizations ranging from Fortune 50 corporations to $10M start-ups – I've learned a lot. I've even written a book that attempted to capture a fraction of those learnings.

Shields Meneley Partners has had a different – and unique – perch from which to observe business and senior business leaders over the last several decades. This singular partnership, comprised of three exceptional people, has advised more than 1500 executives through all stages of a successful career "life cycle": joining new organizations in new roles; taking on broader responsibilities in current organizations; and, leaving organizations by their own choice or because they "were not invited to stay", as one client so elegantly phrased it.

Gail Meneley, one of the co-founders of the business, had always aspired to write a book about this extraordinary journey, but the demands of the business had prevented it. Then one of her clients, Dev Mukherjee, suggested that she invite her clients to write it, and offered to co-author the book.

On these pages, you will find key learnings from people who devoted a thousand years to the business of leading corporations. Read and learn.

Don Perkins was involved in building and leading Jewel Companies, Inc., a food and drugstore chain, during his early career and served as Chairman and CEO for the ten years prior to his retirement in 1980. After that, he served on various Boards of Directors including:

AON; AT&T; Corning Glass Works; Cummins Engine Company; Eastman Kodak Company; Firestone Tire & Rubber Company; Inland Steel Industries; Kmart Corporation; Lucent Technologies, Inc., The Putnam Funds; Springs Industries, Inc., and Time, Inc. At the time of his death in March 2015, he served as chairman of Nanophase Technologies, director of LaSalle Hotel Properties and director on the Advisory Board of Shields Meneley Partners.

Introduction

Gail R. Meneley

More than fifteen years ago, my partners, Hugh Shields, Dan DeWitt and I, joined forces to provide unique services to top executives around the U.S.; advice and counsel on how best to manage and develop their careers to maximize earnings, opportunities, happiness and continued growth.

Every successful executive needs a lifelong career advisor and thought partner, and a highly specialized network of experts to help them better manage their careers and their lives. That is the service we have evolved over the last 15 years.

The need for these services came from some fundamental shifts in business and society:

- Without wading into the hoopla around the "1%" or executive bonuses, it's clear that top leaders can have a greater impact on value creation than ever before. Infrastructure, readily available capital, and technology have led to massive shifts. They created new billion dollar businesses and contributed to the failure of household names.
- The intensity and velocity of business has transformed our lives. We work harder, longer, and are connected 24 hours a day – to our teams, our customers, and our partners. Rapid changes in demand, opinion, and even social and political climates have taken a toll on senior executives' lives, health, and relationships.
- At the same time, there has been a shift of focus to fitness and health. Innovations in healthcare help us live longer, maintain the vigor that drives successful people, and fuels the desire to want to do, learn and achieve more.

- CEOs have greater comfort with risk and a desire for new challenges, which may explain why their average tenure is only three years. They might pull the ripcord, or the organization might pull it for them, as they "move in a different direction".

With few exceptions, our clients have spent their entire careers on the "up escalator". Sometimes there were stumbles in their professional or personal lives, significant or insignificant, in or outside of their control. But in most cases, they dealt with success or adversity in the same way: by focusing on the immediate problem and working to "solve" it.

We believe that life provides a mere handful of opportunities to step back, take a breath, and open the aperture to take in the possibilities that a fast changing world offers. So, our clients spend a few months examining what they enjoy and what is important to them professionally and personally – as individuals, family members and part of a larger community. We then help them revisit what they might have done differently, clarify their philosophy of management and leadership, and identify what they really want to do. Our approach isn't just about the next role – it is about the rest of their lives.

Think about the life-cycle of an executive's career as an infinity symbol. A 40-year career will consist of numerous cycles: you exit one company; enter a new one; are promoted; start to coast; burnout or are "burned" out, you exit…and the process begins again. Most of us could never have predicted the path that led us to where we stand today.

CEOs like statistics; here are ours. Shields Meneley Partners was established in 2003. We have worked with 1500+ executives – C-Suite and direct reports to the C-Suite. Our clients represent all functional roles including CEO, CFO, COO, Finance, Marketing, Operations, Manufacturing, Sales and R&D. Our practice spans all industry and service sectors, large companies and small, private and public. We serve clients all over the globe.

It has been an interesting perch from which to view the world of business and its leaders, so I have been urged dozens of times to write a book about it. But a recent client, Dev Mukherjee, who is also the co-editor of this book, responded to my standard answer "I don't have time" with "So, have your clients write it and you publish it!"

It seemed outlandish, but as we invited the Shields Meneley Partners' family to engage, we realized this was another exciting tool to further our mission. In these pages you will find "Know-How" – the expertise and experience that delivered their success. But you will also learn how they've managed key life and career transitions and crises.

"Know-How" will provide insight and ideas to help you today, and we hope – whether you choose to join our family or not – encourage you to think about your future and create a plan to build your life into everything you want it to be, for everyone who is important to you.

Gail Rafter Meneley
Co-Founder, Shields Meneley Partners
Summer, 2015

Preface

Dev Mukherjee

"If I have seen further it is only by standing on the shoulders of giants"

— Isaac Newton

This has been a surprising project.

After meeting Gail and Hugh (thanks Gene), I could not believe I'd never heard of Shields Meneley Partners, or thought about CEOs needing career advice, coaching and general life planning. I guess I'd assumed if we could run billion dollar businesses, we should be able to plan, manage and deliver everything our investors, teams and families expected of us.

I am grateful for the warmth and generosity of the Shields Meneley Partners' family: the other partners Dan DeWitt and Bob Ryan; the Advisory Board; contributors, reviewers and everyone else who encouraged us along the way. It was incredibly generous of you to give us your time while leading some of the most impressive organizations in the country. Your willingness to share your insights is a credit to you and evidence of your close bond with the firm.

It's very hard to pull together a book. Don't let anyone advise you otherwise, and don't even consider it without an amazing team. With great content from incredible leaders, and a responsive and happy co-editor, this would not have been possible without Katherine Radosky who managed multiple content revisions, kept all contributors informed and on-track, and was always smiling even in the face of impossible deadlines. Katy Kliebhan got us started, supported the initial idea and found our first contributors; and finally, it was Honey Parilla and Richa Bargotra who successfully managed the structure and layout of everything you see here.

To everyone who contributed to the book – including those we couldn't fit in this time, thank you again for your hard work. To Tina Wardrop and Bob Newman, thank you for your feedback. You not only spotted the errors I'd let creep in, but gave us great suggestions on improving content, flow and readability.

To Gail, thank you for agreeing to do this in the first place, and being an incredible partner. This book is a demonstration of the incredible family you, Hugh and Dan have put together over the years, based on the successful service, support and counsel you've provided to possibly the most demanding clients one could imagine. It's been a pleasure to do this, and thank you for all you have done to help me and my family "be all we can be".

I also want to thank my many mentors, colleagues, employees, recruits into the management development programs at IBM, Microsoft and Sears, and my students. Thank you to you all for helping me to work through my own thoughts, and for teaching me much more.

A book takes time, not just to write, but also to think about – I could not have done this without the active support and encouragement of my wife, Sapna, and our kids Rohan and Bryn. You are the reason for all that I do, and the excitement with which I start and end the day.

Dev Mukherjee
Glencoe, July 2015

Section 1

Being the Best

Becoming the Best

Harry Kraemer
Former CEO, Baxter International

Bio

Harry Kramer Jr, the former CEO of Baxter International, has transformed his life and the lives of thousands of others. He moved from Fortune 50 CEO to an esteemed Clinical Professor of management and strategy at Northwestern University's Kellogg School of Management, and is an Executive Partner with the private equity firm, Madison Dearborn Partners. Four years ago he published his first book, *Values to Action*, which addressed the four principles of values-based leadership. He has made 500 presentations on the topic and one common question was asked: How can I put values based leadership into action myself and in my organization? His new book, *Becoming the Best: Building a World Class Organization Through Values-Based Leadership*, responds to the need to extend leadership from the individual to the organization through five stages called "the five bests"—best self, best team, best partner, best investment, and best citizen.

Overview

The "five bests" of becoming a world-class, values-based organization is a journey that follows the path of best self, best team, best partner, best investment and best citizen – all focused on making a *real* difference in the world.

Key Points

- "Your Best Self" is the process of putting into action the four principles of values based leadership.
- "Best Team" means that all team members understand and appreciate what they're doing, why they're doing it, and how it fits with and fulfills the goals of the organization.
- "Best Partner" means that the organization and its vendors and suppliers forge a partnership to enhance the customer experience.
- "Best Investment" is when everyone in the organization contributes to a return for the owners through positive, meaningful actions that support the mission and values of an enterprise.
- "Best Citizen" means moving beyond the organization and its goals to take on the challenge of making the world a better place.

Becoming "Your Best Self"

Becoming your best self is the process of putting into action the four principles of values-based leadership: self-reflection, balance, true self-confidence, and genuine humility. Self-reflection increases your awareness and affirms your commitment to continuous improvement. Balance ensures that you are looking at things from all angles and gathering input from others, especially those with differing opinions. True self-confidence allows you to own your strengths and accomplishments – you *know* what you know. Genuine humility recognizes the value of others and the importance of treating everyone with respect.

Through these principles, you will gain greater self-awareness and self-knowledge, enabling you to pursue the lifelong goal of becoming your best self – and to motivate and inspire others to do the same. Your drive to become your best self will elevate your contribution to the organization and amplify your ability to lead others – starting with yourself.

"Best self" is not about perfection; after all, we're human. But, we can be disciplined and focused on challenging ourselves to be our best rather than resting on our laurels. No matter how good you are, you can always be better.

As you reflect at the end of each day, you may have some regrets. Perhaps you didn't treat someone with respect, or lost your temper. Maybe you acted like a know-it-all instead of truly valuing someone's opinion. In short, your actions were not consistent with your values. When you acknowledge those times you missed the mark, you can recommit to doing your best tomorrow, and every day.

At every phase and stage of your life (personal and professional) becoming your best self is the foundation of your leadership.

Becoming the "Best Team"

When people come together to take on a challenge or accomplish a goal, they form a team. But when people are sharing the journey of becoming their best selves, they create a "best team". Members of the team are self-reflective, they understand themselves, and they embrace a sense of common purpose. They are committed to the overarching goals of the organization and understand how they contribute – individually and together – to the goal and objectives of the values-based organization.

On best teams, everyone's input is valued – even when there is disagreement. Those who must have his or her way most of the time will find that behavior just won't fly in a best team environment. Team members won't tolerate someone who is more concerned about being right than discovering the right thing to do.

A critical component of a best team is a strong values-based team leader who strives to be respected rather than liked. At the same time, the leader understands the critical importance of open, honest, continuous, and transparent feedback that goes *both ways* is not only a good thing to do, it is a moral responsibility to the team and its members. People realize their potential only when they "own" their strengths and weaknesses.

Best teams are critical at every stage of an organization. In a start-up, best teams of values-based individuals often perform more than one function. Each person is crucial to launching and scaling the enterprise. In more mature companies, best teams anchor the organization with values-based leadership. In turnarounds, where dysfunction and in-fighting run rampant, the best strategy is to forge a best team across the company. You must identify those people who collaborate, cooperate, and challenge each other to their highest levels of creativity and productivity and to the greater good.

Unfortunately, even best teams comprised of well-intentioned, hard-working people can focus too narrowly on their own work and forget how it relates to the broader organization. It's the "can't see the forest for the trees" story.

On a best team, everyone see the forest and understands his or her relationship to the aspirational goals of the organization. As each person's view expands, a best team develops a broader horizon and a deeper sense of purpose.

Becoming a "Best Partner"

Best partnerships recognize that we can't do business alone. In order to be successful, we need to expand our "best team" to include external "best partners."

An organization can only attract best partners if they do business in a mutually beneficial way over the long term. This means values and business practices are aligned between partners and focus on a genuine commitment to the organization and its mission of satisfying customers. Best partners are always customer-centric and committed to collaborating to make a meaningful difference in the marketplace.

Best partnership goes far beyond a legal relationship, just as marriage is more than two people whose names are affixed on a marriage license. A best partnership takes a holistic approach and creates win-win outcomes across the value chain, from idea generation to product development.

With a best partnership, all parties know what the other is trying to accomplish, now and in the future. Transactions don't focus on a win-lose dynamic when one party is trying to get the most out of the other. While still competitive, best partnerships are win-win scenarios that understand the benefit of a long term relationship. A best partnership doesn't focus on a single transaction. It's strategic and long-term. It focuses on the success of both parties.

Best partnerships can exist with a variety of partners. For example, an organization and its suppliers can become best partners to enhance the experience and satisfaction of the end user. An organization might also forge a best partnership with customers to identify customer needs for additional products and services.

These relationships are confidential and require a high level of communication, understanding, and mutual trust. Trust and integrity encourage parties to cooperate and innovate. In some cases, they even result in a merger since the tenets of a best partnership are already established and bode well for successful integration.

Best partnerships strive for success of all parties. They are committed to improving performance, differentiating products and services in the marketplace, and improving the overall value proposition. In the process, organizations are transformed and a new paradigm emerges.

Becoming the "Best Investment"

Every enterprise has to be accountable for how it generates a return. While this is certainly true of large, publicly traded enterprises that answer to shareholders, it also applies to private companies that answer to owners, foundations and nonprofits that report to supporters and benefactors.

I would argue that one of the most important things that organizations are accountable for is developing and utilizing their most valued resource – their talent. An organization must be a good steward of all of its resources, but particularly the people who commit their time, talent, energy, and ideas to the success of the enterprise.

Organizations attract the best talent if there is a commitment to developing people in meaningful ways – investing in training, expanding individual knowledge and skills, and providing "stretch" assignments where team members can grow into bigger roles and take on additional responsibilities. Leaders must genuinely believe that talent is the "best investment" and let that commitment drive decisions at the highest level.

Overall organizational performance looks like this: values based leadership = elevated organizational performance and shareholder returns. We measure it by increases in stock price, dividends paid to shareholders, and the ability to attract investment capital.

Sales, revenue and profitable growth are the result of best teams, best partnerships, and people committed to becoming their best selves. With the right people in place, an organization can do what it does best and it will be rewarded by shareholders.

Becoming a "Best Citizen"

Best citizens are organizations focused not only on success, but also on *significance* – making a real difference in the world beyond philanthropy and charity. We think of it as social responsibility.

Rather than expecting others to do the hard work, best citizens, individuals and organizations ask, "What can I do to make a difference?" This puts values into action for the sake of the community, society, and the world.

We often think of large-scale, global problems and challenges and wonder what "those guys" (a gender neutral term) are going to do to solve them. Those "guys" include government, philanthropists, and non-governmental organizations (NGOs). As values-based leaders, we must recognize that we are "those guys".

Becoming a best citizen is a belief that each of us is responsible for making the world a better place in big and small ways. It is a commitment to change even one thing, no matter how small or locally focused.

On a larger scale, corporations will commit money and expertise in areas where they can make a difference. For example, a healthcare company might become involved in global health issues, or a food company might address nutritional needs in a certain area of the world. Such involvement enables corporations to become best citizens by being socially responsible in the communities and countries in which they operate, and to extend that involvement globally.

On a smaller scale, a local company or a group of individuals may support a cause in a particular community, becoming actively involved in fundraising, research, or volunteering. A single person with vision can take on a global challenge. One stellar example is Andrew Youn, co-founder of *One Acre Fund*. After graduating with his MBA from Northwestern University's Kellogg School of Management in 2006, Andrew recruited a team to take on the huge task of addressing poverty and hunger among East African farmers. Today, One Acre Fund serves more than 200,000 farm families in Kenya, Rwanda, Tanzania, and other African countries.

There is no shortage of problems in the world that need to be addressed global, regional, and local. Which one do you want to tackle?

Conclusion

The "five bests" of becoming a world-class, values-based organization is a journey that follows the path of best self, best team, best partner, best investment and best citizen – all focused on making a real difference in the world. Step up to the challenge. This is what values-based leadership in action is all about.

Editor's Note: As with his first, Harry will donate all book proceeds to One Acre Fund to support its work of increasing farm yields and feeding more farm families in Africa. The mission and vision of One Acre is an exemplary illustration of becoming the best to the benefit of self, team, partners, stakeholders (e.g., the donors who "invest" in One Acre's success), and, ultimately, the world.

Additional Reading

Becoming the Best: *Building a World Class Organization Through Values-Based Leadership,* by Harry Kraemer, Jr

Emergency Succession Planning: "What if You ARE the Crisis?"

Laura S. Thrall

President & CEO CureSearch

Bio

Laura Thrall was named President and CEO of CureSearch for Children's Cancer in September, 2012. CureSearch is a privately funded foundation that advances the most innovative cancer research and provides resources and education to all those impacted by childhood cancer. Before joining CureSearch, Thrall was President and CEO of United Way of Metropolitan Chicago, CEO of YWCA of Metropolitan Chicago, and a division director of Campbell & Company, a leading national consulting firm that advanced the broad interests of the health and human services sector. Thrall was a member on the Illinois Governor's Human Services Commission, chaired the Chicago Alliance for Collaborative Effort ("CACE"), and led the Donor's Forum Public/ Nonprofit Partnership Initiative Policy Forum. Thrall served on the Visiting Committee for the Biological Sciences Division and Pritzker

School of Medicine at the University of Chicago and currently serves on the Advisory Council for Northwestern University Medical Center's Cerebrovascular Institute.

The Situation

At 51, I was CEO of United Way of Metropolitan Chicago and experienced a ruptured brain aneurysm that almost claimed my life. The subsequent transition of leadership at United Way affirmed my long-held commitment to thoughtful succession planning. My year-long recovery and re-entry into a new leadership role revealed what it means to be a true leader when title, organization and physical capacity are stripped away.

What Happened

At 6:30 p.m., on August 3rd, 2011, I left the offices of the United Way of Metropolitan Chicago where I served as CEO. It was another routinely long and complicated day. I rode my bike the two short miles to my River North townhouse, quickly changed clothes, grabbed some work papers and headed out. I walked a couple of miles to the California Pizza Kitchen, was quickly seated, laid out my night's work, and ordered a salad.

Thirty minutes later, I was lying in the ER at Northwestern Memorial Hospital a few blocks from the restaurant. A leaking blood vessel in my brain had caused me to lose consciousness at the table, and then exploded into a full-blown ruptured aneurysm. In a blink, I went from being 'in charge' of my organization and my sphere of influence, to being in a coma with a catastrophic brain injury and a dismal statistical chance for survival. If I did survive, my family was informed, the acute nature of the bleed promised to leave me severely incapacitated, physically and cognitively.

In the context of a 'leadership question', the challenge here was not *what* to do in the event of a crisis, but what to do if you *are* the crisis?

In the days that followed, my COO and our leadership team immediately stepped in and stepped up. I have always stressed the importance of succession planning "just in case you get hit by a bus," but had no idea it would apply to me. When I promoted my COO two years before, we talked openly about her desire to eventually lead United Way. The team also consisted of several other women I had recruited to help lead our transformation.

They quickly 'closed ranks' to protect me. While they were aware of the severity of my illness, they didn't have the specific details. My family, including my partner, Kevin, was reticent to divulge information that would weaken the United Way's tenuous transformation, or ruin my chances to regain my position. My sister Katie, a seasoned C-Suite executive, took control of the messaging.

As I remained in a coma at Northwestern, my family faced the matter of whether or not I would survive, and if so, if I could ever function independently. Throughout this time, my United Way team rededicated itself to executing our new strategy, 'Live United 2020' – a ten-year plan to transform communities of greatest need throughout Chicago.

Two months after I was stricken, our board chair, David Speer, CEO at Illinois Tool Works, resigned after receiving a devastating advanced cancer diagnosis. David passed away the following September. The United Way lost its CEO *and* its board chair in rapid succession.

Throughout my six weeks in the hospital, and the subsequent months at the Rehabilitation Institute of Chicago, I continued to believe that I would return to my role despite not being able to walk, speak clearly, or see without an eye patch to disable my double vision. I was confident that I was only a 'few weeks away' from returning to my job.

In late October, my rehab team cleared me to return to work with a *few* accommodations. I could maneuver around my home supported by a walker and newly installed safety rails, and I had been a high achiever on the competency exams they administered in rehab. Clearly, neither qualified me to function at the level a CEO role demanded.

By that December, it was clear that my recovery was many months away. I resigned my position at United Way and my COO took over my role. United Way, and the uphill challenges it faced at the end of the great recession, were no longer *my* challenges. Discovering my next role in the world was my new mountain to climb. And the outcome was far from certain.

The year I spent in recovery taught me more about life and leadership than I ever could have anticipated. I don't wish a brain injury on anyone, but the lessons I learned during the event itself and as I clawed my way back from it—were extraordinarily valuable.

For the first time in two decades, it was just *me*. I realized that when you strip away a fancy position with an iconic organization, what remains is who you are—or aren't—as you redefine who you are as a *true* leader.

Part of my leadership persona had been my presence. Thanks to great genes, when wearing heels I was a six foot tall blonde who could command a room and capture an audience as a compelling and engaging public speaker. But the residual impact of my brain injury was a loss of balance and proprioception (the inability to assess how my body is positioned). Without balance—something we all take for granted—I couldn't remain upright without the assistance of a cane, and relied upon tactile and visual cues. This meant no more heels; no more walking, talking and chewing gum at the same time; no more physical presence. Although I grieved for those things that I had relied upon to demonstrate power and leadership, I quickly realized that I needed to develop and use other, less obvious skills.

One thing was clear: I couldn't reinvent myself in Chicago. My vast network of colleagues and peers would only be able to see what I had lost, rather than appreciate the strength that remained. For this and many other reasons, my partner, Kevin, and I decided to move to Annapolis, MD, a destination we had discovered years earlier as we sailed on the Chesapeake Bay.

Conclusion

Korn Ferry quickly recruited me for the role of CEO of CureSearch for Children's Cancer, a national childhood cancer foundation in Washington DC. Over the last two years, I've learned that my *real* leadership skills reside in my intellect and my management experience – not the public guise that I had led with, and perhaps hidden behind. I now command a room with the power of my words and convictions while I am comfortably seated.

I always recognized that I had strength, passion, and vision acquired through decades of leadership roles. But, I led with my presence, and added content later.

Today, I am comfortable with wisdom that comes from deep humility. Today, my commitment is to fully develop the people around me, not only because anyone can "get hit by a bus tomorrow" – but because it is what *true leadership* is all about.

Suggested Reading

"Succession Planning: Proactive Preparation of Future Leaders", Mary Morten and Joy Wright, *Advancing Philanthropy*, July/August 2010

The Value of Know-How

Dev Mukherjee
Former CEO, Evite

Bio

Currently, Dev divides his time between being a board member, coach, consultant, investor and professor. Previously, he was the CEO of two Liberty Media backed companies Evite – the leader in online invitations – and BuySeasons, a $100M specialty eCommerce and manufacturing company.

Earlier in his career, he became the President of several Sears' business units – including Home Appliances, where he returned Sears to #1 with the Kenmore brand, Toys, Seasonal and Outdoor living; all billion dollar businesses.

In high tech, Dev built and led marketing and business development for the database start-up Ingres, after running marketing for Microsoft's Server platform. Starting in the UK, he spent 15 years at IBM launching new mobile products in Europe, leading early Internet investments and finally the creation of IBM's cloud "on-demand" business, earning him a place in Business Week's list of the "25 Most Influential People in E-Business" and MIT's Technovator award.

His personal academic credentials include an MBA from MIT's Sloan School of Management and a Bachelor's Degree in Computing and Information Systems from Manchester University in the UK.

Background

Wikipedia defines Know-How as "practical knowledge on how to accomplish something". I believe the definition might be expanded to include **experience** that can be used to predict and shape the future; **expertise** that represents deep domain or technical knowledge that translates into a true understanding of the options; and **execution** that takes into account getting things done in the current environment with available resources.

Key Points

- Know-How outweighs any other single factor when it comes to succeeding in today's business, economic and social environment.
- Know-How makes you more valuable to your team and your organization.
- Seek mentors with specific know-How to help you develop your own.
- Credibility is based on experience that allows you to share approaches, ideas, frameworks and plans.
- Expertise is scarce and it takes decades to develop. Seek out true experts and use them to generate options and ideas for execution.
- Execution means enabling and inspiring an organization – frequently customers, partners, and suppliers, too – to work together to deliver the strategy.

What makes experience valuable?

Experience enables pattern matching so that you can better understand what's important, generate options, and predict outcomes. Deep Blue, the IBM super-computer, used brute force to beat the chess grandmaster Gary Kasparov. It worked through every single move and chose the best path. Experienced leaders build up their store of know-how through study and personal experience.

David Brooks, the New York Times columnist, has written about how leaders use this store of experience to identify what's different about a new situation, frequently from large amounts of disconnected inputs, to create options and select the best path.

This experience store can be distilled and shared; research on British Football clubs revealed that managers who played at a high level themselves, raised the productivity of less-skilled teams (skills transfer) and managers with professional management experience raised the productivity of talented players (emotional intelligence and people skills).

Your experience is based on building, searching out, learning from what came before, and turning all of this into your own playbook, to share and refine. This Know-How allows you to get the most from your team, make better decisions, and identify opportunities or obstacles early in the game.

Expertise

"There are no instant experts in chess—certainly no instant masters or grandmasters... We would estimate, very roughly, that a master has spent perhaps 10,000 to 50,000 hours staring at chess positions..."

Malcolm Gladwell popularized what is now known as the "10,000 Hour Rule", but there is significant debate on whether 10,000 hours is truly necessary to achieve mastery. David Epstein, author of the *Sports Gene*, believes that expertise is also based on innate ability.

David Foster Wallace describes Roger Federer's expertise on the tennis court, as happening faster than conscious thought. Expertise here is also pattern recognition in a specific domain, training mind and body to instinctively understand what will work and what won't.

I think we can agree that whether or not you have the right genes, expertise takes time to build. The *New Yorker* noted that cognitively complex activities take many years to master because they require you to experience and process a very long list of situations, possibilities, and scenarios.

So, when building a team of high performers or identifying a mentor, seek out deep domain expertise that has been forged and tested in a variety of scenarios. Some examples included a marketing person who has launched products in different categories, a CFO who has been in corporate Goliaths and startups, or a sales leader who has sold to businesses and individuals. Watch and learn from their reflexes and adapt your style accordingly. The best way I've found to hone expertise is to teach. Teaching will help you check that you have a solid foundation, and can communicate your expertise.

Execution

Research reveals that 60% of employees – including many top executives – said their organizations were weak at execution. Most often companies, teams, even governments fail not because of a flawed strategy, but because they were unable to execute.

Execution – getting things done – is hard. Ironically, the challenge of execution is often an afterthought delegated to a project manager who was often not involved or consulted in earlier decision making.

Execution is related to experience and expertise but there is one fundamental difference: execution is about how the organization as a whole – leaders and followers, partners, suppliers and customers – implements the strategy.

I have identified three types of "Know-How" that drive successful execution:

- **Ensuring individual success**. Every organization is a collection of individuals. If individuals can't succeed then neither can the group. Each person needs a culture that supports their success and clarity about what the organization is trying to do and what his/her role is in reaching that goal.
- **Defining success as the outcome we need to achieve**. All too often teams are focused on short-term projects or activities. If you change the focus to something tangible and measurable, you change outcomes. It is equally important to have the result be externally focused, e.g., improving the customer experience, reducing customer churn, or eliminating slow moving inventory.
- **Building and developing the right teams**. "A" players hire "A" players. Everyone wants to work on great teams where they can learn and win. Hiring is a leader's most important role, yet it is everyone's responsibility. Firms that practice this, e.g. Wholefoods and Google, enjoy the highest productivity and the lowest turnover.

Elements of successful execution can be identified in different ways. For example, a recent *Harvard Business Review* article listed *"17 Fundamental Traits of Organizational Effectiveness"*. No matter how long the list, I think it requires four things: clarity of purpose; a culture that enables individual success; clear communication of goals; and measurement that defines success and drives alignment, and people.

Conclusion

Pace of change, technology, and global competition means that all organizations must deliver better outcomes with fewer resources.

Scarcity of talent is a huge challenge, and leaders must consider the needs of the millennial generation if they are to attract the best and brightest. Command and control, hierarchical management no longer works. The system is too slow and doesn't focus on the personal success of individuals. It must change.

In 2001, a group of software developers created the Agile Manifesto, a new way to run software development projects. This manifesto focuses on individuals, internal collaboration, tangible outcomes, and working closely with customers in responding to change.

Agile has been used to improve many different processes, from building homes to educating people. It focuses on successful execution. Here's an example from Google that shows how things are changing:

[6]On a Friday afternoon Larry Page, CEO of Google, was unhappy with the ads being displayed with Google's search results. Rather than convening a meeting and working through layers of management, he simply posted printouts of the offending ads on the break room bulletin board with "THESE ADS SUCK" in big letters across the top. By 5:05 a.m. on Monday, a group of engineers, not part of the ads team, had posted a solution.

Can you imagine this response in your own organization? Isn't the result reason enough to create a new level of clarity about expectations and outcomes for your team? If execution increasingly trumps strategy, how will you change the way you lead? Get ready for the challenge.

Recommended Reading

"Why Experience Matters", David Brooks, *New York Times*, September 16, 2008 Op-Ed

"Substitution and complementarity between managers and subordinates: Evidence from British football", Sue Bridgewater , Lawrence M. Kahn, Amanda H. Goodall, *Labour Economics* 18 (2011)

"The Role of Deliberate Practice in the Acquisition of Expert Performance" K. Anders Ericsson, Ralf Th. Krampe, and Clemens Tesch-Romer, *Psychological Review* 1993, Vol. 100. No. 3, 363-406

"The Secrets to Successful Strategy Execution", GL Neilson, KL Martin, E. Powers, *Harvard Business Review*, 86, 6, 60-70, June 2008

Jack: Straight From the Gut, Jack Welch

How Google Works, Eric Schmidt and Jonathan Rosenberg

Life Balance

Karl Kramer
President & CEO, Whitehall Specialities

Bio

Karl Kramer has more than 30 years of leadership experience in the food and beverage industry with companies including Nestle, Monsanto and Tate & Lyle. He has served in expatriate assignments in Mexico, Brazil, and Switzerland. He, his wife Elizabeth, and son, Ethan, live in North Barrington, Illinois.

Key Points

- Balance is a goal many aspire to, but find difficult to achieve. Establishing clear personal priorities can help decision making when evaluating options.
- Tradeoffs are a reality; they have consequences. The best you can do is to make decisions consistent with your priorities and live with the outcome.

- You don't need to abandon personal priorities to be a business leader. Having balance in your life can make you a more empathetic, effective leader in today's work environment.

What You Need to Know

Work-life balance is a critical consideration when choosing a job. In the past, the lifetime employment "contract" demanded that senior executives always prioritize work over other personal considerations. That model has been replaced by free agency. This means that you can make your own decisions about how you can best balance your professional and personal life and avoid the Solomon-like choices that affect lives and careers. There are no easy answers. Decisions are complex and "no win" situations can be the rule rather than the exception. That said, as with other things in business, decision making is easier if you are clear about your priorities and if daily choices are consistent with your long-term values and goals. Your game plan will not only be unique, it will also vary significantly at various stages of your life.

Before I share some insights, I want to be clear about my personal bias. I'm not a fan of the term "work-life" balance since it sets work and non-work activities at odds. Most of us spend 50% or more of our waking hours on work-related activities that are often rewarding and fulfilling. I view work as *one* of the key priorities of my life along with my marriage, children and personal time. I pursue a holistic goal of ensuring that the key facets of my life are in relative balance at any given time.

A useful analogy is a four-legged stool that I consciously try to keep from toppling over. When one of my priorities gets "out of whack" the stool gets wobbly. When this happens, I address the imbalance quickly because it doesn't take much to make the stool tip over. And frankly, during my life, the stool has tipped over a number of times.

I'm also not a believer in a "one size fits all" model, and yours may be based on a six-legged stool or a pogo stick. The point is that daily decisions affect long term priorities. For most of my career, I didn't think about priorities because my career was very challenging and rewarding. But, I've made significant missteps that could have been avoided if I had clear priorities.

My early career centered on getting ahead quickly in the business world. At this stage, I spent a great deal of "optional" time at business dinners, company golf outings, a night-time MBA program, drinks with colleagues and the like. My early career prospered, but I was married, and family time and personal time took a clear backseat to making it big in the business world.

My epiphany came about five years after my first son was born. I realized that I could never regain the time I was losing with him, but that I could always find time when he was out of the house to rededicate myself to my career. I shifted my priorities. The result was eight terrific years coaching travel sports, camping with the Cub Scouts, and developing a close relationship with him that lasts to this day.

The storybook ending to the story would be that despite getting the father-son relationship back on track that my career and marriage didn't suffer. The reality is, they both did.

At work, while I continued to deliver results, I wasn't participating in the intangibles that help make or break a career. While the "go-getters" were working long hours and attending regular business dinners, I was on the baseball field or at a pack meeting. My career progressed, but more slowly. On the marriage front, time with my son and my career took priority over my marriage. Ultimately, we divorced. So, the bottom line is that these personal decisions have trade-offs and unintended consequences, so go in with your eyes wide open.

My son was older and I entered a new personal relationship. So, I began to explore options to reignite my career. This time I made decisions based on a balance between my four priorities.

An opportunity to run a business in Mexico presented itself, and my new, adventure-loving wife and I agreed to take the leap. Later moves to Brazil and Switzerland allowed me to carve out a unique set of credentials that led to rewarding executive experiences.

But, we now have a nine-year old son, so I've tweaked my game plan again. I'm much more capable of making the trade-offs necessary to be a successful executive, husband, father, soon-to-be grandfather and, most importantly, a person.

Conclusion

It's easy to allow your career to take over your life. Business leaders "wear" the extreme hours, they work as a badge of honor. Few talk about the results they achieve. Don't fall into this trap. Businesses are measured by results, not the clock. Is "hours worked" listed on *your* annual objectives? That said; it takes dedication and disciplined time management to be an effective business leader. Travel, crises, and uncertain schedules are par for the course. They require occasional trade-offs, but not for long if you consciously work to get back to the balance point as soon as possible.

Having a clear strategy–and a commitment to achieving life balance–has helped me with the challenging decisions I make every day. What's the pay-off? I believe that I'm a better, more self-aware person and a more empathetic, effective business leader as well.

What's *your* strategy?

Ten "Rules" of Leadership

Perry Brandorff
Account Director, Towers Watson

Bio

Perry Brandorff is a seasoned business executive and Board member. He was the President of Consulting for Hewitt Associates, a leading HR consulting and outsourcing business and helped direct the company's profitable growth organically and through global acquisitions. Brandorff's Board experience includes serving on Hewitt's private Board from 1999-2002 where he participated in taking the company public, and on the private Board of Hewitt Bacon and Woodrow from 2002-2008. He currently serves on the Board of Advisors for HighRoads, a private venture-backed professional services firm that provides employee benefits solutions to Fortune 1000 companies.

Key Points

- Walk the talk.
- Surround yourself with the right people.
- Create followership.
- Connect the dots.
- Align your players.
- Guide and direct, don't prescribe.
- You're not always the smartest person in the room...don't act like it.
- Praise in public, criticize in private.
- Remember: passion inspires passion.
- Focus your time and your organization on your client/customer.

In successful organizations, leadership starts with the CEO, but it must be part of the DNA of the entire leadership team to ensure alignment and focus. Although leadership has many elements, I consider the following ten "rules" a clear–not to be confused with easy–formula for success.

Ten Rules of Leadership

1. Walk the talk.

Good companies have a set of clear, shared, aspirational values. If yours doesn't, it's your job to define them. I'm not talking about slogans posted in the cafeteria. I'm talking about values that are reflected in everyone's behavior, every day. As CEO, you must demonstrate these values in everything you say and do.

2. Surround yourself with the right people.

All CEOs need the right people around them. "Right" means those with the appropriate experience, skills and the motivation to succeed... but it also means the right values. If any of your direct reports come too close to the edge on ethics, lose his/her temper, or embarrass people in public, it is *your* problem and your reputation. You are judged by the people who surround you.

3. Create followership.

"You're not leading if no one is following." It is almost impossible to *over* communicate, so talk about the vision and plan with colleagues at every level. Be open and transparent so that you earn people's trust. And not to put too fine a point on it, look over your shoulder occasionally to make sure that others are actually behind you.

4. Connect the dots.

Your colleagues assume that you understand the big picture. Sometimes, they are even right. But, it's your job to connect the dots between the "big picture" and each person's unique role in an organization if you are going to reach aspirational goals. It's the vision thing. Some bricklayers see a wall, others see a cathedral. Your job is to help others see the cathedral.

5. Align your players.

Don't allow members of your team to work at cross-purposes. If there are problems between people, put them in a room until they resolve them. If there is disagreement about the direction of the organization, "duke it out" behind closed doors and insist that everyone leave the room speaking with one voice. If conflict exists on the senior team, trust me: everyone in the organization knows it. And, dysfunctional behavior will follow.

6. Guide and direct, don't prescribe.

People look to you to lead. They may have large, complex projects and approach you for suggestions or ideas, and you can provide high level direction. The problem comes if direction morphs into micromanagement. In other words, if you find yourself telling people exactly what to do and how to do it, one of you is redundant.

7. You're not always the smartest person in the room... don't act like it.

Some people feel that they are the smartest person in the room no matter what the venue or situation. If you are one of them, you're wrong. You may have developed a solid strategy, but it can always be improved by having other brains working on it. Present your original strategy as a "draft". Invite other people's input and celebrate – and incorporate – really good ideas. You will not only improve your strategy, you will also increase the odds of successful execution because everyone owns it.

8. Praise in public, criticize in private.

This advice applies to every part of life: management, leadership, marriage, even parenting. It defines you as a leader. Public praise demonstrates a willingness to share credit and to openly celebrate the accomplishments of others. It's a powerful motivator no matter *what* level someone's role falls on the organizational chart. By the way, can you *even remember* the last time *you* were recognized publicly? Remember how great it felt?

Criticize carefully. Think about it as "feed-forward" rather than "feed-back". Make the conversation constructive, helpful, and future-oriented. Describe what you would like to see the next time in terms of structure, process or outcomes. You want to encourage people to take appropriate risks but with greater insight into how to accomplish the goal.

9. Passion inspires passion.

Members of my leadership team often asked me, "What can I do to inspire my team? I think that may have been the wrong question. The right question might have been "How do I communicate my *own* passion to my team?" Inspiring people isn't just saying the right words and waving a flag. If you don't believe what you're saying, people see right through you. Even if you rely on data and logic to make decisions or shape a strategy, never be afraid to first describe the vision you have for the future of the company and to support the vision with the facts.

I've learned that *real* leadership captures both the hearts and minds of a team, and that has never been truer than the workforce of today.

10. Focus your time and your organization on your client/customer.

If you allow it, 80% of your time will be consumed by people problems *inside* your organization. At the end of a long, frustrating day a close friend put it like this: "Business would be *so* easy without people!" We've all had days like that, and it is very easy to get drawn into the drama that is a part of every organization.

The real question is this: What kind of growth might your organization achieve if 80% of your time was spent focusing on customers and teaching others to do the same? True customer focus is a game changer.

Life Lessons From a Serial CEO

Gary Graves
Board Member,
Einstein Noah Restaurant Group

Bio

Gary Graves has had a diverse, distinguished career as a CEO, COO, Executive Chairman, and Board Member of public and private companies across consumer products and services, for-profit education, restaurants, real estate, and retail, including market leaders Caribou Coffee, American Laser Centers, La Petite Academy, Boston Markets, and Yum! Brands. He has led large multi-site consumer businesses through rapid growth, M&A, diversification, turnaround, and value creation. He is recognized as a strategist and operator who advises companies on ways to capitalize on opportunities that build lasting financial, market, and shareholder value in an era of market complexity, global competitive pressures, and regulatory change.

What I've Learned Along the Way

I've learned a lot of things along life's journey. As I thought about them, none of them were particularly earth shattering but all have proven valuable.

1. Show up early; nothing bad happens when you're early.
2. Listen more than you talk; you'll learn more.
3. Learn how to disagree without being disagreeable.
4. Focus on finding solutions, not placing blame.
5. Bring your boss ideas, not problems.
6. Don't let others define who you are.
7. If you're an operator, don't be intimidated by spreadsheet jockeys.
8. It's OK to be the only sober person at the party.
9. Being smart or having high test scores never guaranteed success. But, a great education lasts a lifetime.
10. Always live below your means.
11. Marry someone with a sense of humor.
12. Don't be afraid to take risks.
13. Praise publicly, criticize privately.
14. When you consider making a move, be sure you're running "to" something rather than "from" your current situation. The grass isn't always greener on the other side; it's greenest where you fertilize it.
15. Play golf; it will ensure you remain humble no matter how important your career.

When You Get Fired

Gail R. Meneley
Co-Founder, Shields Meneley Partners

Bio

Gail R. Meneley is a co-founder and principal of Shields Meneley Partners—a firm that makes great leaders even better through confidential advisory services to C-Suite executives and Boards of Directors in times of transition. She and her partners, Hugh A. Shields, and Dr. Dan DeWitt, have advised more than 1500 top executives from public and private companies from $50M to $50B in revenues, professional services firms and nonprofits. Client companies include Allstate, AT Kearney, Bank of America, Baxter, Booz Allen, Bristol Meyers, CNA, DeVry, Federal Signal, GE, JP Morgan, J&J, Kaplan, Kraft, McDonald's, Motorola, Nokia, Quaker, PepsiCo, R.R. Donnelley, The Tribune Company, and hundreds of others.

Key Points

- Don't assume that no news is good news.
- Establish a values-based philosophy and process to be used for all C-Suite terminations.
- Define the 'right' way to handle sensitive people matters.
- Spell out the implications of doing it the 'wrong' way

What You Should Know

Imagine that you have flown halfway around the world to make a presentation to the Board, but instead of giving the big speech, you get a pink slip. Or, you walk into a routine monthly board meeting at 9, are terminated at 10, and before you can drive home to break the news to your family, the news is on the Internet and a local ABC television affiliate has called your home and asked your 15-year-old daughter how she "feels" about her father being fired?

Although we've all read stories about the callous way in which thousands of people have been terminated each year, as a CEO, you can't assume that your termination will be handled with much more finesse. And not to put too fine a point on it, *every* CEO will be terminated at some point in his/her career because they *did their jobs*.

We've found that Boards rarely confront problems related to CEO performance head-on. With the exception of a handful of top executives terminated 'for cause', most CEOs lose their jobs for the same reasons that other executives do: failure to meet financial targets; failure to execute; or failure to communicate. If tough conversations have not been held along the way, CEOs can be blindsided by the act itself, and humiliated by the way the termination is often carried out—with surgical precision—coldly, brutally, and without preamble or explanation.

No matter how compassionate Board members might be, the first call they will make will be to an attorney about how to do it. Attorneys are hired to avoid risk so they will often advise them to stick to the facts: *"We are terminating your employment with XYZ Corporation effective today. The decision was a difficult one, but it is irrevocable. These documents describe the provisions of your severance agreement. We advise you to retain legal counsel to carefully review the documents. You have XX days to respond. There is no need for you to return to your office. We will have all of your personal effects packed and shipped to your home within two days."*

In our roles as Executive Advisors and coaches, we are often asked to meet with the CEO immediately following termination. Some CEOs are surprised, but knew there was trouble; others are devastated and need help 'getting their arms' around what has happened. In all cases, they have genuine concern about what they are going to tell their spouses, children, friends and direct reports. How will they say it? What *shouldn't be said* in the inevitable calls from colleagues, executive recruiters, and sometimes, reporters?

There are some basic tenets you need to follow to lower the odds that this will happen to you.

1. **Don't assume that no news is good news.** It helps if you have clear, agreed upon performance expectations at the outset, with an official review once a year, and a shared understanding of the consequences if performance goals aren't met.

    But even if those understandings are in place, the Board may not have confronted you about a particular performance issue. But don't be naïve: they noticed. In fact, the less they talk about problems that you and your team know are obvious – like a revenue shortfall – the more concerned you should be. If they don't raise the topic, you should. Avoiding such discussions doesn't make the issue go away; it just goes underground.

2. **Discuss the philosophical underpinnings and the process that will be followed for *all* C-Suite terminations**. The way senior executive terminations are handled says a great deal about the corporate culture. Most terminations are not for 'cause" which means they can be managed gracefully. Legal requirements should be balanced by best practices used by transition experts. This combination will determine the appropriate content and tone for internal and external

announcements about an executive departure. It will also formalize who will deliver this extremely difficult message, what will be said, how it will be said, and whether it would benefit the executive and the organization to have a transition advisor on-site.

3. **What is the 'right' way?** There are many more stories about poorly handled firings than those handled well. As a CEO, it isn't easy to lead complex organizations facing global competitive and economic challenges – particularly when many factors are outside of your control. But, you know that the 'buck stops here'. It is part of the risk/reward formula that comes with the job. As a result, agreeing on an exit strategy during the hiring process, i.e., honeymoon period, protects your interests. Having an agreed upon model for you and your top team will make what is always a difficult process, less disruptive for everyone.

4. **What happens if exits are handled in the 'wrong' way?** If we assume this is not your first 'rodeo', you know that you were associated with your former organization long after you left. All stakeholders – staff, customers, vendors – carefully observe the way in which departures are handled. Other top executives watch how these scenarios play out, and make assumptions about how they will be treated in similar circumstances. Don't underestimate the significant reputational risk associated with an unexpected CEO departure. The goodwill that has been built up over decades can be lost in a matter of weeks of negative media. Market leadership can shift with the loss of a single global customer, so no organization can risk having others think that they treated a departing CEO poorly.

    And as a practical matter, remember that the company will still need you to represent corporate interests in regulatory or legal matters, and to ensure a smooth hand-off of responsibilities to the new CEO. There are the facts written in a file somewhere, and then there are the nuances and issues behind those facts that could cause the new CEO to make rookie mistakes if not fully informed.

Conclusion

A CEO termination ripples through an organization, so handling it with empathy and integrity can help everyone come to terms with this personal and organizational transition event. Not only will you be well-served, but the Board can have confidence that they conducted themselves in an appropriate way.

Creating a Virtual Board of Advisors

Robert J. Ryan
Partner, Shields Meneley Partners

Bio

Robert J. (Bob) Ryan is a global business leader and a partner with Shields Meneley Partners. Bob began his career as an aeronautical engineer and moved to the Human Capital side of the business based on a reputation for bringing the right people together to address issues, facilitating creative problem solving, and designing successful outcomes. He has been in senior leadership roles in businesses ranging from $500M to $5B, including Procter & Gamble, Tate and Lyle, Bombardier Recreation Products, and Griffith Laboratories.

Key Points

- You might benefit from an informal network of people to call from time-to-time for advice.

- Structuring these contacts can make this process more effective for you and your network.
- Your network may never know the role they play as a member of your *Virtual Board of Advisors*.

What You Should Know

In North America and Europe there are a select group of people who never meet, don't even know they *are* part of a team, and yet are among my most important personal and professional resources. I call them my "Virtual Board of Advisors".

I contemplated this concept for almost a decade, and a few years ago finally put it into practice. Interestingly, my Virtual Board's best work occurred during my transition from the corporate world (where I had led the Human Capital side of the business for almost 25 years) to what I've decided to do next. They have never known the important role they play in my career decisions and transitions.

How does it work? I have assembled eight trusted advisors over the years and communicate with them 3-4 times a year. They are a team with a shared objective: to be a critical source of information. I turn to them for feedback, to act as a sounding board, to provide creative input, to offer common sense, and even to play around with crazy ideas.

My eight advisors are diverse by design and include men and women of all ages, geographical locations and professions. The youngest is 34; the oldest, 71. They are from the four corners of Canada/USA, Germany and the UK. There is an HR professional, a country singer, a HR consultant, a senior recruiter, a CEO and an entrepreneur. A couple of the members are retired, several work on their own, and others work for companies. Their diversity clearly helps with the quality and breadth of advice and counsel that I receive.

Key Principles

It must be a two-way relationship. I make sure that each meeting or call fulfills a need for the other person. That could be as simple as buying lunch, listening and/or coaching. I call quarterly even if there is no clear need or objective on my part. It is good to catch-up regularly and "catching-up" is the phrase I use as I set up the meetings and calls.

Imagine the individuals as a team around a table. Even though this never happens, I prepare as if it will. What is the objective of the next round of calls and meetings? What do I want to accomplish? I prepare as if I am going to a Board meeting. I enter quarterly call reminders on my calendar, and spend a few hours preparing for the first call since inevitably, that discussion leads to topics that I may carry into the next call or meeting.

Eight is enough. While there is no magic number, I believe that too many advisors can be a problem to manage, just like any board. I also feel that fewer than five may reduce the diversity and richness of the input. In reality, I probably catch six of the eight in my quarterly meetings.

Keep track and take notes. Okay, I admit it. I started out as an engineer. I *like* tables. I keep a matrix that tracks contact information, last call, input from each member and some personal information. The latter gets the conversation going on the next call. "Did your son make the team?" because you discussed this event in your previous call. I also color-code the input. Crazy ideas (orange) have led to some of the most valuable paths I have pursued.

You are the membership committee. I carefully considered who I wanted on my Board. Diversity was important to me for a number of reasons. I also thought carefully about each relationship. I suppose the Board could flex depending on the need or issue, but I have chosen to stay with the same eight people for several years. I believe that if you tailor the team to the task, you miss out on a unique viewpoint from someone who may not be knowledgeable about the specific issue – but may have related experience that informs your thinking. I also value people who are "fun' to talk to – who are interested and interesting.

There is no need to let each person know you see them as part of a team. I suppose this article lets "the cat out of the bag" for my advisors who read this book. But, I don't think they need to know the structure since it may lead to assumptions about the issue or the team that might be distracting and irrelevant.

Conclusion

This is a simple, effective way to obtain valuable help. It works, it's rewarding, and it develops a two-way relationship based on trust. I look forward to each call because I find that I consistently uncover at least one "gold nugget". With respect to my professional transition, I followed my advisors' advice, took the time to explore options, and made my final decision having received the best counsel from the people I have counted on to have my best interests at heart. It's a perfect fit.

Suggested Reading

Portfolio Life, *The New Path to Work, Purpose and Passion after 50*, David Corbett

Sea Trials, *A Lone Sailor's Race Towards Home*, Peter J. Bourke

Frozen!

Roger S. Hunt
Former CEO, Advocate Bromenn

Bio

Roger Hunt has served as a senior leader in healthcare organizations for more than 40 years. He has led major organizational restructuring and improvement as a consultant and chief executive officer of hospitals and healthcare systems in the United States and Canada. Throughout his career, he has focused on growing quality integrated healthcare delivery systems. A Life Fellow of the American College of Healthcare Executives, Hunt holds an MBA from the George Washington University and BA from DePauw University. He has retired from operating roles but continues to provide leadership and consultation support for local and regional charitable healthcare and arts organizations.

Background

I faced failure as I attempted to bring a new hospital into a growing health care system. I found myself "frozen", unable to conceive a workable strategy. I engaged an executive coach who helped me redefine "failure" and apply that new perspective to my decision making process. I ultimately re-framed the mission of the organization and recommended that the hospital be closed, and its assets redeployed. It was the right thing to do.

What You Should Know

When a CEO publicly invests in a bold strategy that falls apart, it's hard to see a way out. I had undertaken the biggest risk of my career — merging a small under-performing urban hospital into a successful suburban teaching hospital. I sold the importance of expansion to leaders of our health care system and indicated that the acquisition of this hospital was the key to our success.

The first year went as planned. I consolidated governance and management, integrated the medical staffs, and launched an aggressive marketing effort in the new service area. But, by the second year we weren't meeting our revenue targets and all financial indicators were heading in the wrong direction.

As is usually the case, the executive team and the board looked to me, the CEO, for answers. I didn't have them. I was frozen in place for days...and then weeks...and didn't know where to turn. I finally reached out to a trusted coach for help.

CEOs are often expected to have all of the answers, yet they are rarely close enough to the situation to fully understand the issues. Others in the organization "protect" them (or themselves) by not bringing them bad news, and boards don't encourage CEOs to reveal uncertainty or doubt. The expression "It's lonely at the top" is real, and can create an environment where there is no trusted advisor.

A good executive coach can solve this problem. They actively listen, and know how to ask powerful questions. After describing the situation, my frustration, and my sense of failure about not being able to see an alternative, my coach asked: "How do you define failure?" This single question went to the heart of the matter. No individual wants to fail, but if losses continued the hospital would fail too. With my coach's guidance, my brain "thawed" and I was finally able to define a new plan with metrics and incentives. At the next board meeting, I laid out options that allowed the hospital to redirect resources to improve the health of the community.

To my surprise, facing the possibility of failure head-on was both liberating and energizing. It allowed me to openly explore options and strategies with the board and the executive team. The staff and the management team were empowered to develop a plan that would allow us to continue to serve the community even if the inpatient service had to be closed. Three months later, the Governing Board approved the closure of the hospital. The inpatient services were integrated into our larger medical center and ambulatory services for the urban community were maintained.

A key success factor in any change management process is "unfreezing" stakeholders, not only allowing them but *encouraging* them to let go of old ideas and perceptions to support a new direction. By openly discussing the possibility of having to close the hospital, associates could become a part of the change plan. They also had the opportunity to articulate and celebrate the valuable contributions the hospital had made over more than 100 years.

Knowing that regulatory approval for the closure would take nine months to a year, we used that time to involve and communicate with all associates. The management team developed a detailed closure plan including a comprehensive outplacement plan to support those who would be displaced. Staff involvement and early communication made it easier for associates to find opportunities within our suburban medical center and at neighboring city hospitals.

All of the 630 associates who desired employment were successfully placed, and the media credited the hospital for redefining itself in a very "over-bedded" part of the city. On the day the hospital closed, its rich history was celebrated with a community event attended by former staff, volunteers and community members.

Conclusion

A successful leader recognizes that the art of management should begin with managing your own actions and reactions. A coach can hold up a mirror, ask powerful questions, and help you overcome the isolation that is inherent in any top role. Releasing your own "frozen" perceptions and fears and voicing them to a trusted coach and advisor is a tremendous asset.

Recommended Reading:

Management at the Speed of Change, Daryl R. Conner

Leading Change, John Kotler

Coaching Questions: *A Coach's Guide to Powerful Asking Skills,* Tony Stoltzfus

How to Execute a Successful Career Transition

Jan L. Davis
Board Member, Megalytics LLC

Bio

Jan Davis is a retired CEO and active board member for companies that sell software, analytics, database and digital marketing, and information products and services to industries including retail, real estate, financial services and insurance and direct to consumers. She serves on the boards of directors of ShowingTime.com, SEAL Innovation and GSP Marketing Technologies and on the boards of advisors of multiple companies, including Megalytics, Market Vue Partners, Spring Metrics and Three Ships Digital. She is the President of Triangle Angel Partners, an Executive in Residence for the Blackstone Entrepreneurs Network, and on the Investment Committee for the non-profit Launch Place Seed Fund. She was the CEO of ShopperTrak RCT Corporation, EVP and Business Unit President at TransUnion LLC, and was a marketing consultant.

Key Points

- Professional transformation takes time, preparation and hard work.
- Financial preparedness and a wide, strong network are critical.
- Networking with a generous attitude – what YOU can do for others is much more effective than the alternative.
- Opportunities often come from unexpected connections.
- Change of location, industry, or title is challenging and results aren't immediate.
- Remaining open to change pays off.

Background

My career was on an upward trajectory. The "first phase," learning to operate in a fast-paced, entrepreneurial environment, landed me as co-founder of a venture-backed business. The "second phase" included eight years as an Executive Vice President and business unit President at TransUnion. Then, the Board of ShopperTrak recruited me to join the company as President and CEO. After my first year, revenue and profit growth were exceeding expectations, and our Board was very happy.

I decided to join the Board of the Illinois Technology Association (ITA). I didn't think I would be seeking a new opportunity in the short term, but knew that it was important to have a professional network in place. Less than two years later, Scott Woodard, a member of the ITA Board and the CEO of Showing Time, invited me to join his Board as an Independent Director, my first such role. He had been a participant in the CEO Roundtable I had facilitated for the organization.

Two years later, ShopperTrak's revenue took a hit when retail customers began conserving capital – a prescient move given the economic collapse the following year. I believed that continued investment in information products was critical to future success but was unable to convince the Board. Within months, they decided that the organization needed to go "in another direction" under a new CEO.

I fully expected to land another President and/or CEO position quickly and threw myself into networking. I was in active conversations with three companies when the economy went into free-fall. A fellow CEO from the ITA Roundtable had also recruited me to help him raise money to expand his business into healthcare with the idea that I would join the executive team of this expanding business once fund raising was concluded. Needless to say, the recession dried up investment capital and senior leadership roles.

I networked throughout the following year. I didn't land another full time position, but did develop a spreadsheet with 600+ connections, their origins and subsequent contacts, and hundreds of situations where I made introductions for others. I continued my work with the ITA, networked at semi-annual meetings of the Alumni Council of UNC Kenan-Flagler Business School, and had many referrals from friends and business acquaintances. By late 2009, I was working with three companies in California, two in Chicago, and one in the Raleigh/ Durham area of North Carolina. I found that I truly enjoyed the work on a Board of Directors or Board of Advisors, and realized that I could do it from anywhere.

In January 2010, tired of the dreary Chicago winters, I heeded the advice of a fellow Showing Time board member and real estate investor, and put my house on the market. The good news is that I received an acceptable offer the first week in March; the bad news is that since I wasn't expecting it to move that quickly, I had to make housing decisions—fast. I briefly considered Florida but weighed its benefits against the thriving tech community in the Raleigh/Durham/Research Triangle of North Carolina. The desire to be nearer my aging parents in NC tipped the scale.

I had a deep network in Chicago after 14 years there. Although I had grown up in North Carolina, I had not lived in the state in 30 years and had never lived in The Triangle. Networking during the previous 18 months had yielded some contacts in the entrepreneurial ecosystem— entrepreneurs, investors, accountants and attorneys—but I needed to invest more time and effort into the community to truly uncover opportunities.

Now, a little over four years after the move, I'm well-established in this "third phase" of my career. It has been an interesting transformation from leader, mentor and team builder to "nose in, fingers out" Board service. I serve on three private company Boards, one in Chicago, one in Raleigh, and one in Clearwater, FL. I was elected to the Board of Triangle Angel Partners, a firm with $2.8 million in committed capital and eight companies in our portfolio, named to the Executive Committee in 2012, elected President in 2013. I serve as an Entrepreneur in Residence for the Blackstone Entrepreneurs Network and on the Investment Committee for a $4 million non-profit seed fund in Danville, VA. Advisory or consulting roles in The Triangle, Chicago and Kansas City fill up the rest of my work week, leaving time for travel and family—particularly my parents who are now 88 and 92 and still in their own home. The work is satisfying and energizing, and if I follow in my parents' footsteps, I'll be an active board member, angel investor and mentor till my 80s.

Lessons Learned

- Be prepared financially for any professional transition, but especially a transformation which may mean living beneath one's means.
- Build connections and relationships throughout your career, not just when you need help.
- Lead with generosity. Never leave a meeting without asking how you can help.
- Remember that opportunities often come from the least expected quarters.
- Be open to change. A new location, new occupation, new colleagues and friends can make this new chapter energizing and rewarding.

So You Want to be a PE Portfolio Company CEO?

Hugh A. Shields
Co-Founder, Shields Meneley Partners

Bio

Hugh Shields is a co-founder and principal with Shields Meneley Partners, a boutique provider of executive consulting services that works exclusively with senior executives to drive business results through improved individual and team performance. He has extensive P&L and strategy development experience in industrial, commercial, and consumer markets. He has held senior management positions in a variety of industries including professional services, specialty chemicals, electronics, and electrical products. He has focused heavily on successful private equity portfolio company CEOs as client interest has shifted to this investment model.

Key Points

- Private equity firms aren't like public corporations. Understand these differences before you proceed.
- A solid fit with the culture and values of the firm is critical.
- Understand the firm's business model and investment criteria.
- Understand the firm's compensation model.
- Spend time with other portfolio company CEOs to confirm the daily reality from the sales pitch.
- Determine how you measure up against the personality profile of a successful PE operator.
- Be objective: calculate your odds for success.

We've spent almost 20 years advising 1500 senior executives through successful career transitions. During that time, one of the most significant trends has been client interest in moving from large public companies to small/mid-cap private firms. Here's what we've learned.

Why all the interest?

Private equity firms came roaring out of the recession with billions of dollars on the sidelines and a need to generate investor returns. What PE firms used to accomplish through the magic of financial leverage now depends on having exceptional executives who know what strategic and operating levers to pull to drive performance. So about the time corporate demand dried up, PE began knocking on the doors of corporate executives and received a warm welcome.

Public company executives face extraordinary pressure – growing investor demands, stifling governmental regulation, and board members asserting control in unprecedented ways in a post-SOX and post Dodd-Frank environment. When an opportunity presents itself to "downsize" to a smaller company e.g., $200M to $500M+, they want to seize it. And let's be frank: private equity presents an opportunity to build significant wealth by betting on your own ability to succeed in a risk/reward environment.

What we see.

Private equity firms have differences in culture, levels of management oversight, and ROI expectations. Corporate executives who don't understand those differences are often caught flat-footed. They don't adjust quickly enough and don't make it to the finish line. Since PE executives generally trade significantly lower cash compensation for an equity stake that will pay out at exit, they are particularly hard hit if they fail. They find themselves without a job and with less net worth than they had going in.

Don't misunderstand. There *are* successful exits that generate millions, but those outcomes aren't the norm. Valuations are high; PE firms have to invest, or return money to investors; and sometimes that can result in unrealistic expectations about EBITDA. If you're a savvy executive, you will perform your own diligence on any deal you consider and not bet your future on someone else's analysis. If you are skeptical about the underlying business model, strategies, or market assumptions, walk away.

There are three points of entry.

There are three ways to engage with private equity: bring them a deal; begin as an operating partner, executive-in-residence or board member; or fill an open position.

Bring them a deal. There is no better way to get a PE firm's attention than to bring in a specific deal or a compelling deal thesis, like a possible consolidation strategy to unlock the synergies of acquisition targets. Show market size, competitors, targets, executive team differentiators, operating plans, exit strategy, etc. You only need to develop a high level (about two pages) business/financial model about targets and financial synergies, because they will scrutinize your financial model in great detail later. If you are aware of a private company or an orphan public division for sale, say so. If you have an existing relationship with the CEO or founder, say so. It's a huge advantage.

Be candid up to a point, but keep in mind that this is *your* intellectual property so make sure you guard the specifics as you shop around for the best firm for you. In other words, show them that you know the industry, how the model will make money, and a number of potential sellers and targets. But don't give away the store. At the end of the day, make sure they need *you* to make the deal happen.

Even if things are on track, you'll sit on the sidelines much longer than you think. At the front end, the PE firm will expand your deal thesis, conduct necessary research, and identify and reach out to target companies that could be potential add-ons. If you can consummate the deal based on the initial platform target, you've done well. But experience shows that there may be several companies you're targeting in parallel and this can take a while to play out. Realistically, unless everything goes perfectly—and how often does *that* happen?—the process can take one to two years. Prepare yourself and your family both psychologically and financially for that eventuality.

And one more warning, despite everyone's good intentions, deals can blow up at the very last minute. Understand on the front end the PE firm's criteria for closing—or withdrawing—from a deal. If you don't, a deal could be executed that will result in unreasonable terms and expectations.

Accept a role as an operating partner, executive-in-residence, or board member. Private equity partners are incredibly talented financial engineers and risk mitigators, and they do everything they can to squeeze the risks out of a deal. CEO failure is a huge risk since it threatens operating synergies, market opportunities, and exit timing. Firms often move senior executives into CEO roles after they've had a chance to see them in action as an operating partner, executive in residence or board member. You earn your way in by being successful in the roles leading up to that seat. They get to know you, you get to know them, and you've had an inside look at the company. Many C-Suite executives don't have the patience to wait on the sidelines for a year or two. Do you?

Fill an open position. This is the most direct, certain, and fastest path to a senior operating role in a portfolio company. Many PE firms have a vetted "stable" of qualified candidates to move into these roles. PE firms view operating talent through a very tight industry and functional lens. Their view is if you have been successful in the past, you can do it again. Don't waste your time pushing your candidacy if your experience isn't a *direct* match. They simply will *not* consider you if your background isn't a true fit.

The successful PE profile

There are specific competencies and characteristics that PE firms seek – and sometimes assess for – in portfolio company leaders:

- Entrepreneurship – think like an owner
- Action-orientation
- Decisive
- Autonomous
- Focused on results
- Critical thinker
- Deep financial acumen*
- Deep domain/industry knowledge
- Relationships with potential targets and strategic buyers
- Lean operator
- Vision to see a clear exit strategy and timeline
- Hands-on operating skills
- Financially motivated
- Willingness to invest personal net worth

*Pay careful attention to this one. PE partners are financially sophisticated and you need to speak their language and understand how they think about a business. You aren't just managing a P&L as you often run a corporation or a division; you're managing a balance sheet. Highly leveraged environments require cash management skills and focus.

How do you know if you are right for private equity?

At first blush, you might think you have all of those competencies. Be brutally honest with yourself about this. We've learned that most executives from larger pubic companies really *don't* have the appropriate competencies–particularly when it comes to infrastructure support, pace, and comfort with risk. If you really want to pursue this option, do a deeper dive with an executive assessment from a reputable firm like Shields Meneley Partners. We have experience assessing senior executives for PE portfolio companies, and can identify strengths, weaknesses, and potential blind spots. Also, reach out to partners you know in PE firms that focus on targets different from yours. Invite them to lunch and ask for candid feedback about your fit. It could save you time and frustration.

Conclusion

Private equity is not for everyone. Make sure you have the patience, stomach, risk profile, and competencies. You'll also need confidence in the business model, and comfort with the firm partners with whom you will be working. You don't have to be friends, but it is important to be aligned regarding ethics, management style, and a shared understanding of the end game. If you make the right decisions, and the stars align, the world of private equity can be lucrative and rewarding. Let us know what you decide.

Traits for the Top –
It's About Collaboration

Daniel J. DeWitt, Ph.D.
Partner, Shields Meneley Partners

Bio

Dan DeWitt is a psychologist and partner with Shields Meneley Partners, a boutique provider of executive consulting services that works exclusively with senior executives to drive business results through improved individual and team performance. He is a certified Master Coach with more than 20 years of experience providing executive assessment and coaching for organizations in all stages of development, from start-ups to Fortune 100 companies.

Introduction

In over 30 years of assessing executives for senior level positions, there have been a few traits that have remained constant indicators of success. In nearly every decade, new competencies are viewed as equally necessary. Early in my career, organizations were emphasizing intelligence, defined as critical thinking and strategic agility. With the 1995 publication of Daniel Goleman's book *Emotional Intelligence*, EQ was added to desired competencies.

It wasn't until the mid-2000s that companies began asking if I could assess an executive's ability to collaborate, and the demand for that skill has remained high over the last decade. I have been brought in by companies to assess the entire senior team's collaboration skills. Shields Meneley Partners has also been asked to develop programs to improve executive collaboration so that team members "play well in the sandbox." As organizational structures become more virtual, operating across business units, time zones and continents, collaboration will remain a highly valued characteristic.

Key Points

- In the past, organizations were looking for critical thinking skills, followed a decade later by emotional intelligence. Now **collaboration** is the "coin of the realm".
- Collaboration is an activity where people work together for a mutual or shared goal.
- Collaboration is a "must-have trait" for a successful executive.
- Most top executives are *not* collaborative.

What is this collaboration trait?

Collaboration is working together to achieve a mutual or shared goal. The first type of collaboration is when people work on parts of a project and the sum of the efforts produce the desired outcome. This can be seen when creating a new cell phone and various engineering units, i.e. design, mechanical, software, etc., work on their unique parts to build the phone; or in the music industry when one person is responsible for the lyrics and someone else is responsible for the melody like Lennon and McCartney worked together to churn out hit after hit. In this type of collaboration people often work independently, but are dependent on each other to achieve the desired outcome.

The second type of collaboration is when people work simultaneously on an issue; they are sharing ideas, skills and experience, often in real-time, to produce a solution or product. This type of collaboration can happen when several people work on a draft in Google Docs, or when a team is discussing potential solutions to a problem that only one team member "owns". In all forms of collaboration, the key feature is that everyone who has an investment in the end product agrees to work together to achieve a successful outcome.

In my experience, executives view collaboration as the first type–owning part of the process and agreeing upon the mutual goal of helping a company achieve greater success. Yet, I think boards and CEOs are really asking me to assess the second type of collaboration since higher performing executive teams require senior leaders who know how, and who welcome the opportunity to work in close collaboration with peers.

Why is executive collaboration so critical?

CEOs realize that no single person is smart enough to navigate the increasingly complex business and economic environment. They gain deeper insight and make better decisions when they hear from more members of their team rather than a single person closest to a particular issue. Donald Hambrick, in his seminal work on the topic, describes the difference between a group of executives and a team: "A top management group qualifies as a team to the extent it engages in mutual and collective interaction." More progressive CEOs want higher performing executive teams because they believe that the whole is greater than the sum of the parts.

Why isn't collaboration more common among senior executives?

Baby Boomer executives have spent 25 years focused on their own and their team's achievement and are often involved in turf wars jockeying for power. They find it uncomfortable and a bit threatening to share openly with their peers in a collaborative process. In the book, *Teams at the Top*, Jon Katzenbach wrote that few senior leadership teams function as a team because organizational structures do not encourage it and incentive plans do not reward it. Often, executives run their own region, function, or area and rarely reach out to others to solve problems.

Today's senior leaders are highly motivated by achievement. They do not naturally share resources, e.g., people, ideas, etc., if someone else might benefit or get credit and they will not. They may be right. If the wrong incentive systems are in place, one executive could make a bigger bonus or suddenly have the inside track on a promotion. Most incentive structures are built to reward individual achievement, so CEOs must make sure to balance rewards for individual accomplishment and collaborating with peers.

Executives complain that it takes longer to accomplish things when they are expected to talk with their peers to make a decision. This is both resistance to the idea of collaboration, and the truth. As one senior HR executive recently told me, "It *does* take longer to make decisions and it *can* be a pain, but it's not a choice. Collaboration ultimately results in better decisions, and it is expected of an executive leadership team."

By the way, collaboration is *not* the same as consensus. Executives who try to achieve consensus will soon see that decision making will become glacial, and execution will be significantly delayed. A CEO should have several goals: to encourage and reward collaboration; to achieve buy-in and input from various members of the team; and to drive towards a decision where everyone feels heard. In a 2010 *HBR* article, *"The Best-Performing CEOs in the World,"* Ibarra and Hansen emphasized that one way to promote greater collaboration is to refuse to get stuck in debate. The best CEOs do not expect that all decisions will derive from collaborative thought, nor do they think that collaboration should cause everyone to feel happy with the result.

How do you become more collaborative?

First, you have to want to work with someone and believe that sharing as part of a high functioning team achieves better outcomes. Personality type is also an important and necessary factor in collaboration. Extroverts often find it easier to collaborate than introverts because they are typically energized by interacting with others. Yet, introverts can become better collaborators if they focus on learning from others and feel appreciated for contributing their ideas. Further, when the CEO and performance systems reward collaboration, both extroverts and introverts will be more likely to commit to the collaborative process, even if it is difficult. Many executives realize that this type of interaction is more fun. Everyone has everyone else's back and positive work relationships develop.

Second, an executive must have a genuine interest in *learning* from others. Being a good listener is important, but being more interested in learning from someone else, rather than showing-off what you know, is essential to improving collaborative skills.

Third, each team member must agree to collaborate with the expectation that collaboration will be reciprocated by our peers. The CEO must be clear in these expectations and the culture should reinforce it.

Conclusion

Senior leaders must make collaboration a "best practices" trait because the need for it is here to stay. Millennial employees have grown up sharing their experiences, thoughts and ideas online through various forms of social media. They want and expect to have a voice in decisions and to hear what others think. The good news is that collaboration will be a natural skill for younger staff members. And, as they move up the ranks, collaboration will be the norm and better decisions will result.

Suggested Reading

"Are You a Collaborative Leader", Herminia Ibarra and Morten T. Hansen, *Harvard Business Review,* July 2011

Teams at the Top, Jon R. Katzenbach

Strategic Leadership: *Top Executives and Their Effects on Organizations,* Sydney Finkelstein and Donald C. Hambrick

Leading in the New Abnormal

Timothy J. Gardner
Former EVP, Illinois Tool Works

Bio

Tim Gardner served as Executive Vice President of Illinois Tool Works Inc. (ITW) from 2009-2014. ITW (NYSE: ITW) is a 100-year-old Fortune 200 global diversified industrial manufacturer of value-added consumables and specialty equipment and related service businesses. The company focuses on profitable growth and strong returns across global platforms and businesses. ITW's revenues totaled $14.1 billion in 2013, with more than half of these revenues generated outside the US. Tim currently serves on several boards of directors.

Background

As the world continues to slog its way out of the 2008 recession you often hear people say, "Get used to the new *normal*". That doesn't go far enough. We are in uncharted territory. Economic recovery and future success will demand a level of strategic and tactical agility that most business leaders have never tested in real time. Get ready for a rocky ride.

Key Points

- Today's leaders must be agile in an environment of rapid change when they are more "unknowns" than "knowns" in our decision frameworks.
- Technology and social media have opened the world to a level of personal and organizational scrutiny never before seen.
- Business leaders must communicate clearly, often, and well to anticipate, adapt, and respond to rapidly changing products, services, competitors, and markets.

Leading in the new abnormal

The "new abnormal" impacts how executives lead. In the last seven years alone, corporate strategy has been redefined by:

- Increasing reliance on – and uncertainty in – global economies
- Strains on global alliances that have been relatively stable since World War II.
- Technology enabled consumers that relate to brands in a totally different way.
- Technology that changed how we make products, where, and how we calculate paybacks.
- Changing aspirations and expectations of young leaders entering the workplace.
- Rapid changes in how people prefer to communicate.

The hackneyed phrase "the new normal" has been part of the vernacular since the beginning of the 2008 recession. It inferred that standard economic assumptions and business practices had been turned upside down, but that we had some understanding of what the new normal would look like. As change increased exponentially, we recognized that nothing was "normal" about the landscape that was shifting around us. Here are a couple of examples.

Communication: Internal communication has traditionally been top down – CEOs defined the vision for the organization, explained why it was important, and described how the organization would achieve it. External communication – aside from that prescribed by financial or legal disclosures – tended to be inside-out with minimal feedback or dialogue. In other words, the organization in most cases communicated in a prepared and scripted way to a selected audience.

These traditional models are up for grabs. I'm on the Board of a non-profit organization rethinking its communication strategy because donors and users want information in a different way. They are using new channels to create a dialogue and seek input on issues and decisions. Users want to engage *emotionally* and to *feel* like they are part of the organization. In the case of this non-profit, they want to feel immediate gratification that they are part of a great and important cause. This powerful shift will have a huge impact on our organization. It enables us to increase engagement, transform fundraising, and promote volunteerism to drive the growth and health of our volunteer organization. However, it is a new experience for many of us who are less comfortable with the power of social media.

Major CPG companies have been leaders in adopting new communication channels to actively engage consumers. They have also learned that their employees want to engage with management in a more direct way so that they *feel* part of the organization and its' strategic direction. Executives must be willing to communicate in new ways, embrace innovation at all levels, and engage end-users in ways that challenge traditional thinking.

Technology: Today, a new product investment decision needs much more planning and diligence. Leaders need to formulate contingencies and "what-ifs" before making a large technology investment.

In an industrial company, a new product typically takes two to four years from conception to commercialization. R&D expense is only the beginning. A technology investment must be highly differentiated and represent meaningful value to earn customer and supplier acceptance. The decision matrix for technology investments becomes more complex and entails greater risk than ever before. New products need to be tested through part of the value chain including distribution, consumer use, and sustainability. Yet, these are necessary investments that contribute to the growth, innovation, and health of the organization.

Summary: Today's leaders need the agility to navigate a rapidly changing environment. It's a bit like white water rafting. You generally enter at the mouth of the river where the current is slow and predictable so you have time to anticipate the actions you need to take. You quickly round a bend and are confronted with whitewater, massive boulders, and savage cross currents that take all of your courage and skill to navigate. There are waves of economic, business, and market challenges that require the same level of courage and skill from our business leaders – but there is also game-changing opportunity.

Successful navigation through the "new *abnormal*" will require executives and teams to share a vision of the future, embrace the risk and opportunity that is part of it, and to *feel* that the outcome is in their hands. Welcome to the New Abnormal!

Section 2

Creating
the Most Value

What Investors Look For

E. David Coolidge III
Vice Chairman, William Blair & Company

Bio

David Coolidge is Vice Chairman of William Blair & Company, a private investment banking and money management firm. In addition to serving as the firm's CEO from 1995 to 2004, he has dedicated his 35+year career to financing and building prosperous companies throughout the Chicago area—start-up ventures, mergers and acquisitions, corporate and financial restructuring, and public/private debt and equity financing are his targets. Coolidge has served on numerous boards including, Kmart Holding Co., Coverall of North America, Duluth Trading Co., the Securities Industry Association, and the National Association of Securities Dealers and is currently a trustee for Williams College, the University of Chicago and Rush University Medical Center, an advisory board member for Northwestern University's Kellogg Graduate School of Management, and a member of the Civic Committee of the Commercial Club of Chicago.

Key Points

- First time entrepreneurs usually source capital from savings, family and friends who bet on whether they trust the competence and integrity of the *person.*
- Professional money managers that source larger amounts of money bet on whether the *deal* is a good business investment.
- Investment professionals ask: Where is the deal coming from? Why am I so lucky? How good is the management? How good is the business? What's unique about the business? What's the competitive landscape? What's the financial model? How do I exit?

Background

Looking for equity capital can be daunting to entrepreneurs or managers who have little experience approaching sophisticated investors. That's one reason why first time entrepreneurs usually source capital from savings, family and friends. In these situations, investors are generally backing someone they know and who they believe has a decent chance of making a go of it. These investors don't have rigid return on investment criteria and don't ask for voluminous business plans.

The game changes when a company needs to approach professional money managers. As the amount of money increases, so does the level of difficulty obtaining it. The good news is that larger capital raises can attract intermediaries who will write the business plan, organize presentations and introduce the company to appropriate investors. Respected intermediaries add value in a variety of ways. They act as a first screen in the vetting process and other sophisticated investors know that intermediaries don't take on assignments unless they believe the deal has merit.

So what questions do investors ask when approached about an opportunity?

Where is the deal coming from? What familiar touch points will the investor see so that he/she is willing to take the next step? If the deal is coming from a known intermediary or a known professional contact, an investor will assume the company is run by a competent, trustworthy person because they trust the person making the introduction.

Why am I so lucky? Every opportunity will be presented as a huge winner, but the investor needs to believe he/she is a logical backer based on industry experience, geography, or some other link. Investors have to be convinced that a deal plays to their strengths and experience and that they will have as much insight as someone else. The investor wants to feel he or she has an edge, just as the business needs an edge to succeed.

How good is the management? In higher risk private investments company leadership is crucial to success. Investors need to be totally convinced that management is smart, able, experienced and driven. If a full management team is not in place, the investor will want evidence that the entrepreneur has the contacts and charisma to convince others to join the team. The more reference points an investor can get on the ability of the leadership team, the better. Will the team be investing, too? Are they risking a meaningful portion of their own net worth? Has the team built a business in the same field? Does the entrepreneur have vision and passion, *and* the flexibility to adjust plans if the marketplace doesn't react as predicted? Stan Golder, who founded the private equity firm, GTCR, often said he would rather invest in an "A" management team in a "B" market than a "B" management team in an "A" market.

Is it a good business? The size of the market opportunity is important, but it's also helpful if the market is growing. Investors are attracted to businesses that have the wind at their backs and operate in growing markets. Determining the size of the market is important and not always straightforward if it is a new offering. Steve Jobs always dismissed the question about market size when introducing a new Apple product because he believed that people wouldn't know they wanted the product until it was made available to them. And he was right. But you aren't Steve Jobs. Investors need answers to the market size and growth question. Is it an "A" market or a "B" market?

What is unique or special about the company? Patentable proprietary technology usually means a company has something that nobody else has. But, it doesn't guarantee success since competitors with similar technology can claim their technology is different and may be willing to run the risk of infringing. Warren Buffett describes his businesses as being surrounded by moats that keep others from getting into their space. It may be a patent, a dominant brand, market share, or even a proprietary manufacturing process or distribution system. Taking on businesses with very wide moats can be challenging. Creating businesses with very wide moats can be very rewarding.

What is the competitive landscape? Even though a business looks like it has an edge, a proprietary technology or some other way of distinguishing itself, investors will look very closely at actual and possible competitors. If a new business is challenging a larger entrenched competitor, the investor will look at how that competitor reacted in the past to new entrants to their market. If the large company has reacted strongly with litigation and/or price wars investors will be wary and worried, especially if the large company has significant resources. If a new business is going after a new product or service an investor wants to know who else is trying to enter the same market. Venture capital moves quickly into an emerging area and will often fund multiple companies to take advantage of the opportunity. The first mover advantage is not a sure path to success, but it helps. Being the tenth player in a new area is not going to be very attractive.

What's the financial model and how will the business perform from a growth and ROI standpoint? If the business has a track record, an investor can analyze its financial characteristics and have a good sense of what might happen if additional capital is infused. Investors shy away from the proverbial hockey stick projection with rapidly rising growth rates and expanding margins if there is no track record to support it. Actual performance is rarely as good as projections, so running a conservative and an optimistic case can determine different capital requirements under those scenarios. It is helpful to raise more money than you think you are going to need, or to have backers who can invest more if building the business takes longer and requires more capital than originally anticipated. It's like building a building. No one builds without a contingency fund even though architects and builders believe they have thought of everything. Building a business over time means unforeseen challenges will present themselves that generally require money to overcome.

Conclusion

There will be many, many more questions than the ones featured above. Each investor has his own check list and ways of evaluating opportunities. Someone might want to see your college transcripts or delve deeply into your personal life to look for things that could distract you from paying attention to your business 24/7 or to turn up undisclosed problems in your history. Some investors employ psychologists to evaluate managers. Many will want to meet your family to make sure they are supportive and enthusiastic about what you are proposing to do. Be prepared for anything and everything.

So, you may be asking yourself "Do I really want to go through all this pain and suffering just to have a shot at raising money?" It's a good question. And, sometimes running an existing public company can be easier than being an entrepreneur. With a public company, you call up ten investment bankers and have them pitch for the business.

On the other hand building a business with the help of private capital can be immensely rewarding, both financially and psychologically. With that in mind, however, there is one more question the investor will ask.

How do I get out? You need an answer for that one too.

So You Want to Buy a Business?

Philippe Martin-Monier
Chairman & CEO, ICE

Bio

Philippe Martin is the President and CEO of ICE, a leading company that provides water preparation and filtration systems to the beverage industry. Martin, an expert in issues and opportunities related to water and waste businesses, was the Senior Vice President of Research and Innovation with Veolia, the global leader in water and waste management. He focused his team on business needs including water purification, water distribution networks, waste water treatment and recycling, waste gaseification and recycling. He developed a "smart city" program with Singapore, Mexico City and Lyon.

Earlier in his career, he turned around and built environmental services companies from $10M to $500M in Europe and the US. Philippe graduated from Ecole Polytechnique Paris and the Massachusetts Institute of Technology in Cambridge, USA. He received his MBA from La Sorbonne in Paris.

Key Points:

- How to make your decision to buy.
- How to define your project/target acquisition.
- How to develop a clear plan that opens the door to sellers and investors.
- How to ensure the right fit on all levels–on both sides.
- It will happen only because of your commitment and energy.

Making up my mind

When I left a senior role in a very large global corporation, my initial thoughts were to find a similar job in a similar company. It took me a few months to discover that this wasn't what I wanted to do in the next stage of my life. Meeting with and exchanging ideas with people who bought a business after a successful career in a large organization was key in my decision process: all the people I met wished they had done it earlier in their careers. The assessment feedback I received from Shields Meneley Partners also provided important insight. I realized that I am an "intrapreneur" – someone we laughingly refer to as an entrepreneur who relishes creativity and innovation – but who prefers to risk other people's money! So, I first needed to overcome my reluctance to put all my financial eggs in one basket.

Defining my project

I wasn't interested in buying a business just for the sake of owning something. I wanted to identify a market need and find a business to address it. My first idea was to provide a new range of services associated with water piping networks for municipalities and industries. Having a clear business idea helped open the doors in the world of business acquisition: target companies and their owners, financial institutions, private equity firms, and business brokers.

Finding the right fit and being flexible

After four months, I was introduced to ICE, a company dedicated to providing water preparation and filtration systems for the beverage industry. I visited ICE and it was a "coup de Coeur" – a great personal fit with the company, its culture, its challenges and opportunities. ICE needed an experienced leader/owner with a strong background in water-related businesses, with significant international experience, and good relationship skills—someone *exactly* like me. And, it was an exciting opportunity to grow ICE from a technology leader to an industry leader.

Although ICE didn't match my original idea exactly, having a clear idea/angle was very useful in the discovery process.

Empathy is the key to connecting with the seller

Many interested buyers had far more capital than I had. But, I worked with a highly respected financial advisor who gave my offer credibility. But money was only part of the sell. I had to convince the largest individual shareholder and CEO that I understood his pride in the company he had built over 25 years, as well as his concern that the future owner shared his commitment to long term future for the business. After many open, long conversations I finally reassured him he could trust me with his company. Frankly, I was surprised by how important this relationship was to the success of this transaction. We celebrated over dinner and champagne on my first visit to ICE which just happened to coincide with my birthday which I viewed as a good omen.

Nothing moves until you push

There are quite a number of things that have to happen at the same time…operational due diligence, negotiations with the seller, raising capital, and dealing with the banks to secure the LBO debt.

Having been part of a very large organization I was used to business deals moving very slowly. I also had staff to help carry the load. When you are trying to buy a company, you touch every part of the deal, and nothing moves until you push. It is the difference between playing soccer as part of a team that allows you to rest a minute when you need to, and playing tennis where you have to push and hit every single ball.

Here are a few things that I learned…

- After 30 years in the company and 15 years as the CEO, the seller was convinced that he had a jewel. It took time and diplomacy to show him a slightly different picture.
- Warranties and Representations is a difficult document to negotiate; it can be a significant stumbling block with individual sellers.
- There is broad diversity among individual investors. Some are highly risk averse and focused on the short term; others have long term visions with high trust.
- How people deal with their money reveals a great deal about their personalities.

Preparing the transition

Equally sensitive is your approach to the senior staff and employees of the company.

- When the seller talks to his employees about selling the business, it is a key milestone and represents a very strong commitment.
- The sooner you can tell employees what's coming, the less anxiety there is about their roles. After all, this transaction represents not only a new owner, but a new boss, and a different future.
- Provide an opportunity for employees to speak their mind about the future of the business – their hopes and concerns. You might want to hire a consultant to have these conversations, to ensure confidentially, and to provide common themes.

Next Step

Walk the talk, and do what you said you would do.

I am writing this article only days after the deal closed. There were surprises both good and bad, and many more to come. But my enthusiasm and excitement about the opportunity is intact and I am eager to take my company in new directions.

Daniel Burnham, the famed architect of the spectacular Chicago lakefront once said, "Make no little plans. They have no magic to stir (wo)men's blood ..." With that in mind, our mission is to transform a technological leader into a business leader that serves the beverage industry and ensures better water quality around the world.

I'll let you know how we do.

Leadership Styles
Require Guiderails

James L. Madara, MD
CEO, American Medical Association

Bio

James L. Madara, MD, is the CEO of the American Medical Association (AMA) and an Adjunct Professor at Northwestern University. An accomplished academic medical center physician, medical scientist and administrator, Dr. Madara, began his career at Harvard, ultimately serving as tenured Professor and Director of the Harvard Digestive Diseases Center. Subsequently, he was the Timmie Professor and Chair of Pathology and Laboratory Medicine at the Emory University. From 2002-2009, Madara served the University of Chicago as the Thompson Distinguished Service Professor and Dean of both the Pritzker School of Medicine and the Biological Sciences Division, later adding the role of CEO of the health system.

Key Points

- Having a defined leadership style is critical, but it needs to be *yours*.
- "Anchor phrases" can serve as guiderails to keep your actions and reactions authentic, consistent and predictable.
- Guiderails ensure that decisions are made that are consistent with your – and your organization's values.

What You Should Know

What's your leadership style? Styles come in a variety of forms – organizational, financial, strategic, and operational – and still others steeped in the elements of emotional intelligence. Recent studies suggest that no single style is the key to success. Rather, it is your ability to adapt your style to different situations and personalities that provides a different angle or fresh perspective.

So, how do you stay true to yourself and "keep the keel even" while deploying differing styles for specific challenges? How do you ensure that your style is seamless and predictable to those around you?

Experts in behavioral science and management can tackle those broad questions. I simply want to provide my short cut that helps define the "guiderails" for the field on which leadership is played. I, and others I've shared it with, find this approach helpful.

The method is to identify anchor phrases that serve as consistent conceptual guiderails for behavior and decision-making. Regardless of leadership style, these guiderails are consistent, and behaviors/decisions among the team are more predictable. This also helps you be clear and consistent despite changes in organizational environments.

The guidelines I've outlined below have served me well in settings ranging from University leadership, hospital/health-system COO and CEO roles, and as the CEO of a large, complex national professional organization. These roles require traditional business metrics such as ROI, R&D spend, and regulatory compliance, but are made more complex by the difficulty quantifying given initiatives driven by organizational mission. This complexity makes it even more important that leaders be predictable and consistent in their behavior and responses.

The overarching framework is 3-5 phrases that capture "guiderails" that are consistent with your beliefs then internalize them so that you have a pre-conditioned response to each difficult decision. Though the guiderails below are mine, they are intended to illustrate the concept for you.

1. ***Don't fear being caught in the truth.*** Everyone faces embarrassing circumstances during his/her career. If you make a lot of decisions, some will be brilliant; others "boneheaded". Simply own up to it. Explain the process and the logic you applied. Don't shade the truth or attempt to deflect blame to someone else. Just tell the truth. This guiderail greatly simplifies management. No time is wasted trying to keep track of varying stories, and time and energy are directed to the important things. More importantly, you develop a reputation for integrity.

2. ***Take the high road.*** Although this sounds subjective and ill-defined, I've been surprised by how helpful it is. When you face a decision point, it is usually quite clear which path(s) are within this guiderail. Just simply recite it as part of the thought process.

3. ***Long term trumps short term.*** If the largest portion of your day is spent on short term problems, it wastes your time and signals the organization that the long term strategy can be derailed by short term issues. At the end of each day, clearly define how much time was spent on the long term. If it's too little, change it.

4. ***Life is too short.*** At the end of the day, were there moments of humor enjoyed with those around you? Does your environment have a bias toward productivity *and* fun? If not, think about how you can create it.

Conclusion

These are my guiderails, and you will have your own. Make sure they are authentic and consistent with your core values, beliefs, and leadership style. I think you will find that they help you keep your balance even during turbulent times when decisions are critical and time is of the essence.

Recommended Reading

"Leadership That Gets Results", Daniel Goleman, *Harvard Business Review*, March 2000.

"15 Ways to Identify Bad Leaders", Mike Myatt, *Forbes*, October 18, 2012.

"The Focused Leader", Daniel Goleman, *Harvard Business Review*, December, 2013

Customer Loyalty – Are You Missing Out?

Donna Samulowitz
Founder & President, Brand Connectix

Bio

Donna Samulowitz is a long time practitioner in the areas of brand building, strategic marketing, and sales excellence. She founded Brand Connectix to focus on the need for measurable results generated by branding, integrated marketing, customer experience management, customer loyalty programs, and sales performance.

Prior to founding her firm, she served as SVP of Marketing & Sales for USAA Financial Services Association where she enhanced brand architecture, launched the first national advertising campaign, and led innovations in marketing and sales. She also served as President and Chief Marketing Officer for Erickson Living, the nation's largest developer of large-scale retirement communities; Executive Vice President and Chief Marketing Officer for Cardinal Health; and VP of

Customer Loyalty for Whirlpool Corporation where she transformed the company's go-to-market strategy.

Key Points

- Customer Loyalty Programs sizzled a decade ago, attracting strong corporate investment. When the economy tanked, those investments tanked with it.
- Creating a customer centric culture is more important now than ever. If you aren't in dialogue with your customers, you can bet your competitors *are*.
- Social media has shifted the power from the corporation to the customer. Product reviews, blogs, video testimonials, and other viral communication, can make or break a new product or a corporate reputation.
- One thing hasn't changed: *Customers still need products and services that meet their needs and solve their problems.*

Five Lessons Learned

Astute corporate leaders recognize that customer loyalty is the key to success in *any* economic cycle. When a clear strategy is executed across an organization, loyalty programs deliver short term results and pay long-term dividends. In the Whirlpool Corporation Annual Report, the CEO declared, "Customer Loyalty . . . it's just the way we do business."

1. Define how Customer Loyalty (CL) impacts business goals.

Whirlpool Corporation and other manufacturers of durable goods have sales cycles from 7-10 years. Whirlpool's definition of CL includes the acquisition and retention of customers. And, CL behaviors were defined by purchases within and across categories – laundry, cooking, refrigeration, etc. This ignited market share and shortened the sales cycle within brands to two years. Now CL is relevant across 15 global brands.

2. Marketing doesn't "own" CL. It's part of every leader's business.

Some business leaders think they can toss the CL strategy over the wall to land in marketing's "house". The fact is that CL cuts across most functions in an organization. Every leader and front-line manager makes decisions and takes action every day that impact loyalty. Here are a few examples:

- **Customer Service**. One brand's definition of a stellar service experience is different from another's. At Whirlpool, CL results drove a branded call center approach with new metrics by brand – tighter service appointment times for one brand – lengthier conversations about appliance cooking capabilities for another.
- **Manufacturing.** Paying attention to the smallest details can make a difference in customer perceptions. Whirlpool discovered that if manufacturing labels on the *back* of machines were crooked, the overall perception of quality dropped and affected CL scores.
- **Legal.** The language used in customer documents can positively impact customer experiences merely by translating "legalese" into language that customers understand.
- **Human Resources**. Your hiring profiles affect customer experiences. Potential recruits who exhibit skills and attitudes like "friendly, helpful, empathetic", can have a measurable impact on customer loyalty.

3 Improving Customer Loyalty often requires organizational transformation.

When embarking on a CL strategy, organizations that have been driven by R&D, manufacturing, or product may require a total transformation. Other organizations may only need to improve customer focus in specific areas. In all cases, sustainable change is best achieved when it is a systemic, consistent program.

Whirlpool used a customer "embedment" process that included six areas addressed in the transformation:

- **Vision, goal and definition setting.** What is the end state you desire and does that vision instill passion among the employees?
- **Leadership accountability.** What role, responsibility, behavior and actions do you expect leaders to have?
- **Resource requirements.** What people resources—internal and external—are required? Do you have adequate capital to fund the change?
- **Communication.** Who, how, what and when will you communicate to keep the troops informed and motivated along the way?
- **Processes and tools.** How will you integrate new processes and tools into other systems so you don't overwhelm the organization?
- **Rewards and recognition.** What types of *meaningful* rewards can we provide for those who drive this change?

4. What gets measured gets done.

Sustainable improvement is achieved by a CL measurement system. Hit or miss approaches risk poor performance, and may be viewed by employees as a "flavor-of-the-month" idea they can ignore. There are many approaches to measuring CL. Whichever approach you adopt, measure it annually and define the *drivers* of your overall loyalty metric.

Be sure to integrate your CL metrics into employee and leadership objectives. Variable compensation can incent the right behavior. At Whirlpool, we learned to roll this out slowly after change management was embedded and we had a few successes addressing customer requirements.

5. Don't expect overnight results.

Today's business environment is skewed toward short-term results. Creating and cultivating lifelong relationships don't work that way. You can attract new customers in the short term, but sustaining those relationships year after year takes a commitment to a strategy that drives improvements across and into the organization.

When we launched the CL transformation at Whirlpool, the CEO optimistically projected it might take 18 months. He quickly learned that with 54,000 employees around the world, it was going to take much longer and require an ongoing commitment. We did capture quick wins along the way in terms of improvements in products, customer services, and programs. But the *real* payoff came over time when customers used their wallets to demonstrate their passion and loyalty.

Conclusion

A strategy that ensures consistently exceptional customer experiences that drive loyalty takes real commitment. That commitment is based on the value CL brings to each and every brand. If you "take care of customers, they will take care of you" epitomizes the improved business results that a loyalty strategy delivers.

Here are three simple steps to get started:

1. Define CL as a priority relevant to your brand's success.
2. Commit to long term, transformational change.
3. Execute a measurement system to determine current state.

Recommended Reading

Chief Customer Officer: *Getting Past Lip Service to Passionate Action,* Jeanne Bliss; a discussion of customer centricity crossing functional lines within an organization.

"5 Keys to Building Trust with Customers" by George Taylor, President Beyond Feedback, http://customerthink.com/five_keys_to_building_trust_with_customers/

EQ Trumps IQ

Ron Hodge

Former Partner, Booz Allen Hamilton

Bio

Ron Hodge is a business leader with over 30 years of professional consulting experience. As a Senior Vice President/Partner at a $5B management consulting firm, he championed "intrapreneurship," successfully leading start-up businesses and driving rapid growth and diversification of new lines of business, service offerings and key market segments. He is a trusted advisor and expert in business performance and technology. Ron is currently working on his Ph.D., and serves on the board for businesses and educational institutions.

Key points

- People are your most valuable asset.
- Recognize the value of a great coach.
- Value "EQ" as highly as IQ.
- Put together teams that play well together.

A good friend and mentor used to remind me to think of our firm as a team, not a family. Why? From his point of view, a family inherits its members and can be blindly loyal despite obvious strengths and weaknesses. A team on the other hand, plays its "best athletes". When players are no longer performing, they are replaced with better players with observations like, "Times change, we need the best talent on the field."

I bought into that point of view for a long time, and although the principle is a good one, I think it's incomplete. Here is how I'd improve upon it.

Recognize the value of a great coach. I'm a professed sports junkie, and have enjoyed the highs and lows of college and professional teams all my life. I view sports as a good analogy for business. Some teams land five-star recruits year in and year out, but don't win enough games to be contenders. Other teams take less-touted, skilled players, and turn those teams into champions.

The difference is a *great* coach. Good coaches can take skilled people and teach them to play at the top of their game. They share their knowledge and experience, mentor, and serve as a model by doing the right thing. They encourage players to try and fail, but usually in a controlled, low risk environment with appropriate support.

Great coaches take a different approach. As they assemble their teams, they consider the alchemy and fit of each player as part of a *team* and then evaluate team strengths and weaknesses. This approach allows them to change things up depending on the competition, the play, or the environment. Although they create and communicate the overall game plan, they also listen and learn from player feedback and action on the field or the court.

Value "EQ" as well as IQ. Business is full of very smart people, and I have been fortunate to work with many of them. Each was considered "gifted" in some discipline or specialty that helped pave their way to senior positions. Unfortunately, their IQ sometimes got in the way. They spent too much time seeking the purest solution and were often intolerant of others less "gifted." Many of these executives derailed, since top executives need both EQ and IQ to achieve long term success

In my experience, people who rely solely on intellect may be strong *managers*, but they are rarely strong *leaders*. Managers follow routine, repeatable tasks; direct others through numbers or rule-based decisions; and use a formula they invent or adopt. Within that limited framework, projects can often be completed and deadlines sometimes met.

But in today's business environment, being smart is not enough.

I view Daniel Goleman's book, *Emotional Intelligence*, as a must-read for anyone in the business world. According to Wikipedia, *Emotional Intelligence (EI)* is the "ability to identify, assess, and control the emotions of oneself, of others, and of groups". Put simply, it is the ability to understand yourself and other people, and to manage others based on that insight. In my experience, it is EQ not IQ that provides greater and more sustainable value to an organization. Leaders with high EQ understand the importance of the social dynamic and can harness the synergy that is part of a team. They enhance the performance of others by helping teams navigate obstacles, become more resilient to failure, and rebound from setbacks.

The tougher question is whether emotional intelligence can be taught. In my experience, some people may improve at the margins, but in most cases, you either have it or you don't. Tests for emotional intelligence offer some insight, but they aren't a litmus test for business success. CEOs with high EQ can build team emotional intelligence by demonstrating their own ability to listen, respect the team dynamic, mediate fissures within groups, and celebrate successes along the way.

Put together people who play well together. In his book, *Good to Great*, Jim Collins refers to the importance of getting the right people on the bus, but also getting them in the right *seats* on the bus. The complex mosaic that comprises a strong team is comprised of people who get along, are self-motivated, help one another, share a common passion and vision for excellence, and are willing to go the extra mile to get there together.

How do you make sure you have the right folks "on the bus"? The best approach I've found is annual 360° performance reviews using surveys or interviews with an employee's subordinates, peers, and superiors. One firm I worked for invested deeply in this process and it paid off. Employee assessments were discussed not only with senior leaders or their immediate team, but also with leaders of other teams. This approach gave a full picture of the organization's total human capital, and revealed not only skills, but someone's ability to work with others.

Some firms place little if any value on whether a person contributes to overall team performance. They perform "lifeboat" drills and throw people overboard based on core skills proficiency alone. This results in individual performers competing with each other for attention or position. They are innately insecure which can lead to irrational and sometimes unethical behavior and they have no support within the organization. They ultimately fail, but can create significant disruption and dysfunction during their tenure.

Conclusion

As a CEO, always remember that people are your most valuable asset. The best technology, the most sophisticated intellectual property, and the strongest business model can still be trumped by an organization that develops and motivates smart, passionate, empathetic people who represent your organization to your customers every day. Use a holistic approach to ensure that your strong individual contributor also has the ability to be a strong team player and a valuable colleague.

Taming the Leadership Aspects of Technology

Robert J. Moore

CEO, LGIMA

Bio

Robert Moore serves as CEO of Legal and General Investment Management of America, a Chicago based Institutional Asset Management subsidiary of Legal and General UK. Previously, Robert was President of LPL Financial with oversight of the company's primary client-facing functions. Robert joined LPL Financial in 2008 as CFO before being named President in 2012. Prior to LPL Financial, Mr. Moore served as CEO and CFO at ABN AMRO North America and LaSalle Bank Corporation. Mr. Moore has a Bachelor of Business Administration in finance from the University of Texas at Austin and a Master of Management in finance, marketing, and international business from Northwestern University. He holds the Chartered Financial Analyst (CFA) designation.

Anyone in a management or leadership role has responsibility for creating conditions for success. Providing support, guidance and insight to help team members fulfill their personal ambitions should be weighed as you set priorities and align actions.

It is important to recognize that in many ways, technology creates the most effective and effcient environment for an enterprise. At the same time, that very efficiency can divert attention from practicing the fundamentals of communication that build relationships and enable trust and collaboration. Every business is replete with examples of poorly crafted emails that wasted time, energy, and goodwill.

I was surrounded by technology at a very young age, so have no fear or phobia about it. Productivity enhancement tools like Client Relationship Management (CRM) systems or sophisticated Data Management (DM) are impressive. But, I am a skeptic when technology – email and basic presentations – replace person-to-person communication. My hypothesis is this: the quality of decisions being made today is in no way superior to what existed before the Internet or 24/7 connectivity. No doubt the volume and speed of decision making is greater, but that points to more noise – not necessarily better outcomes.

With that, here are some ideas to consider as you create your road-map for leading your team or organization in a high tech world.

Top Ten Ways To Tame Technology

1. Have all team members deposit their phones, iDevices or laptops in the center of the table at every meeting. No multi-tasking allowed.
2. Remove the bcc: function from whatever email system you use – it is fundamentally dishonest.
3. Set up an automatic reply message in email that blocks all cc: messages and asks the sender to resend TO: you if it is that important. CYA is not a cultural trait you should support.
4. Set boundaries for the time of day messages can be sent. Eliminate weekend messages completely unless there is a true emergency. A good rule of thumb is no messages before 7 a.m. or after 7 p.m. in

each person's local time zone. Save messages to a Draft folder if you want to get ahead of the game, but don't send them until 7 a.m.

5. Use the Subject line to call out what action is being requested or what point is being made.

6. When prioritizing IT projects, focus your review and analysis on capacity utilization rather than cost. Meeting the budget but failing to complete key projects is a bad tradeoff. Complete a few projects fully and well–including training and change management–instead of completing more projects poorly.

7. Ask every member of your team to consider picking up the phone or walking across the hall before hitting "send" on any email message. This has the win-win effect of reducing email traffic and improving relationships.

8. Make it clear that any email communication viewed as acting out passive aggressive behavior won't be tolerated. Email has become one of the most insidious forms of cowardice in business today.

9. Require that key assumptions in every PowerPoint presentations be listed at the very front of a short deck along with the answer to this question: "Why is this presentation being made?

10. Try introducing Email Free Fridays (EFF) and enjoy what happens next!

Raising Money for Capital Intensive Businesses

Jim Benak

Co-Founder and Partner, Tetzlaff Law Offices LLC

Bio

Jim Benak is an executive, public company general counsel, trial lawyer, entrepreneur and author. He has 30 years of experience primarily in transportation and manufacturing as both a legal expert and an operating executive. He was an executive at United Parcel Service and Union Pacific Railroad, and has represented other transportation companies in private practice, including Burlington Northern Railroad and Chicago's Metra commuter railroad. He served on the Board of Directors of Union Pacific's positive train control development subsidiary, and the Board of Directors of the NCAA College World Series.

Key Points

- Capital-intensive start-ups pose significant short-term risk.
- Risk is a four-letter word to capital markets, and especially venture capital.
- If possible, reduce your operating leverage and your risk in the short term.
- Use a two-phase approach to raising capital: venture and project capital.

What You Need to Know

When I started at Union Pacific, our Chairman and CEO was Drew Lewis. Before coming to Union Pacific, Mr. Lewis had been Secretary of Transportation in the Reagan Administration. Before that, he had been trustee of the bankrupt Reading Railroad. Mr. Lewis knew a thing or two about how railroads make, or don't make, money.

One of his first observations at Union Pacific was that railroads were a difficult business to manage because of high fixed costs. But he also realized that once you cover fixed costs, marginal costs were nominal and the profit curve was almost straight up. Not surprisingly, he concluded that there were two ways to cover fixed costs: increase revenues or decrease costs. Management was giddy about the simplicity of the solution until they realized they weren't really familiar with how to do either.

Flashback to 1975 and my comparative economic systems class: My instructor was brilliant, a Marxist at heart (who actually looked a little like Karl Marx.) He was focused on subsidies and price supports for the railroad industry to offset extraordinarily high fixed costs. I suggested that he move the curve out so that revenue from increased demand covered fixed costs. "Ah", he said, "you're trying to trap me with the logic of supply and demand."

Back to 1985, my guess is that less than a handful of industry leaders even knew what a free market was, much less how to navigate it. What they did understand was that increasing revenue was going to take too long, and in the short run, they were all in deep trouble. So we focused on the short term slashed costs, and remade a business.

I recognize that railroads aren't start-ups, but like any other capital intensive business you need to closely manage costs and increase revenue. In 2013, the industry made $13B in capital expenditures – roughly the GDP of Iceland. Union Pacific's ROE was 20.5% which shows that when you strengthen a business through smart capex investments, you can attract capital.

Here's a Personal Case Study.

I made dozens of presentations to potential private equity and venture capital investors to fund a capital-intensive transportation business. Our business plan was solid: the company filled an underserved niche; the only competitor was woefully inefficient; we could dominate the niche and foreclose competition; it was unregulated; it had nominal execution risk; we had a well-known transportation company as a potential partner; we had a management team of smart, seasoned C-Suite executives; and the business was projected to return 44% on shareholder equity. We couldn't get arrested.

So why do venture investors avoid capital-intensive start-ups?

The reason is *risk*. High fixed costs that management can't control. Venture capitalists aren't prepared to accept that kind of risk.

The majority of successful venture investments have been "capital light" – defined as investments of ≤ $30 million before commercial scale is achieved. In 2013, 79 of the 98 VC backed exits were in the capital light information technology sector.

Google and Tesla are great examples of how risk shapes investor attitudes. Google is seen as capital light. The company raised $25M before its IPO; was profitable in year three; and generated net income of $1.4B in year seven. If Google is capital light, Tesla is the opposite.

Tesla lost $396M in year seven, and more than $1B as 2014 drew to a close.

VCs have concluded that they aren't very good at "picking winners" in capital intensive investments, so they've lost interest.

If we are all dead in the long run, capital-intensive businesses may not see many more start-ups.

The only way to have a robust industrial sector is to minimize perceived risk. Here's one approach. Think about funding your business in two phases with the first phase designed to *position the company for phase two*—additional investment.

Avoid the phrase "proof of concept". POC implies far more uncertainty than VCs like. Instead explain that phase one positions the company to attract additional capital so that early investors can exit. The magic word is "scalable". Start on a smaller scale and ramp up to create an *operational* two-phase approach.

Here's what I've learned: Investors often lack the background to judge your ability to start and run a successful business. So what you have to be good at is pitching your idea and *raising money*—very different skill sets.

The good news is that your business plan can be pretty light on fundamentals if your goal is only to raise money. How Web-based start-ups can raise billions of dollars and not generate a profit, ever, remains a mystery.

Conclusion

Investment horizons are short in the VC and PE worlds. Use the two-phase approach to position your business to increase your odds of success.

For capital intensive start-ups, structure the business to reflect a "critical mass" early in the game to attract another round of funding. Most importantly, remember that this is *your* baby; that *you will be around in the long run* to make sure that your business succeeds.

Here's what I tell my son: good things rarely come easily or quickly. This isn't about a new Jaguar in your garage. It's about a business that will be around for generations, making money, creating jobs, and contributing to the economy.

It's a worthy battle, don't you think?

Conflict Resolution and Enterprise Risk

Jim Reiman
CEO, Aerofficient LLC

Bio

Before founding Aerofficeint – including creating and patenting the key technologies – Jim was Chairman and CEO of EBT Mobile China, one of the largest retailers of cell phones in the country. An accomplished attorney, he received his JD from Northwestern University and BA from Columbia University, and is also a graduate of Kellogg's Advanced Executive Program.

Key Points

- Reputation and relationships are increasingly important assets.
- How an organization handles inevitable disputes with customers, partners and employees impacts reputation and relationships.

- Many companies do NOT have a strategy to deal with disputes.
- Improper handling of a dispute can have broad and costly results as Toyota experienced in the "runaway car/sudden acceleration" problem.
- Legal responses to conflicts are expensive, unpredictable and can further damage reputations and relationships.
- A well prepared strategy – as implemented by The Toro Company – can significantly reduce cost, time and risk.

What you should know

- Alternatives to "calling in the lawyers" like arbitration and mediation are an important part of a company's risk management strategy.
- Conflict's true cost is much greater than the cost of defense/ prosecution.
- Additional costs include fees for lawyers and expert witnesses plus damages and penalties if the suit is lost.
- The opportunity cost resulting from management focusing on legal proceedings is immeasurable.

Background

Resolving conflicts with employees, customers, vendors, and communities is an integral part of a company's risk management strategy since reputation is one of a corporation's most valuable assets. An *ad hoc* approach to conflict management is just too risky since negative perceptions affect sales, profitability, and market valuation.

Directors must ensure that a conflict resolution strategy is in place, and how the success of that strategy is defined. Is it reducing litigation costs? Resolving conflicts quickly? Reducing negative publicity? Who in the organization makes those decisions?

In today's closely connected world, social media offers unprecedented opportunities to connect with customers, enhance reputation and build brand. On the other hand, anyone with a computer or smartphone and a "bone to pick" is a potential reputational threat that can have substantial financial consequences.

How a company responds to conflict–the tone, the people assigned to resolve it, and the communication channels used–impact reputational risk. Even the smallest matter can "go viral" and escalate into a public dispute or crisis.

Consider the Toyota response to the "runaway car/sudden acceleration" problem. The company initially denied that a problem existed. When presented with overwhelming evidence, the company blamed its customers–the drivers. This response was exacerbated even further when Toyota issued technical explanations "proving" that their vehicles weren't defective.

Crisis management experts will study the Toyota case for a long time to come, but fundamentally, this was a conflict. Customers claimed a product defect; Toyota disputed it. Customers wanted Toyota to take action and compensate them for their injuries; Toyota wanted to maintain the *status quo*. Had Toyota had an effective conflict resolution strategy that weighed reputational and litigation risks, the response might have been different.

Americans often "call in the lawyers" when there is a conflict–a costly and time-consuming approach. Arbitration and mediation are far less costly. The real cost of a conflict is not only the costs of defense or prosecution. It is shifting management's focus to winning/defending a conflict rather than building a profitable business.

Business conflicts are rarely isolated events and are often a by-product of vague corporate policies, or isolated decisions made by engineering, purchasing or marketing. A conflict resolution strategy must be one that removes ambiguity and clarifies the propriety of given conduct or business decision.

The Choice of Arbitration

Arbitration leads to private, binding conflict resolution. Parties select a neutral arbitrator to hear evidence and arguments and to decide the conflict. The decision is binding and the winning party may use traditional courts and law enforcement to enforce the decision and award.

While less formal, arbitration proceedings are much like court hearings. The parties are usually represented by counsel who present evidence, call witnesses, and provide arguments. But, there are major differences that impact the choice of a particular conflict resolution strategy.

In arbitrations, formal rules of evidence don't apply. Decision makers hear all relevant evidence; material facts can't be excluded based on legal technicalities; and motions and the discovery process are limited.

Arbitration decisions are usually rendered promptly–and are less costly–since arbitrators are required to render their decisions within 30 days of the closing of the hearing. As we all know from headlines or our own experience, there can be months between non-jury trials, the conclusion of a hearing, and a final court decision.

Arbitrators are chosen by the parties and while many may be lawyers, they don't have to be. The most common and important quality adversaries seek is expertise in the subject, along with language skills, cultural knowledge, and specific technical knowledge.

Except in very limited circumstances, federal and state statutes prohibit the review of arbitration decisions which means that decisions are certain and final. Appeals are accelerated and must be decided within 30 days of filing the last brief. In a traditional court setting, the appeal(s) filed by the losing party can drag out for years.

In most cases, arbitration also leads to the correct result since traditional court decisions are made by over-burdened judges or lay juries comprised of people who often lack the skill and experience to fully understand the complexities of a business conflict.

Another reason to consider arbitration is that unlike judicial proceedings, arbitration proceedings and records are *not* open to the public and only the parties themselves are allowed to disclose what occurred.

The Process of Mediation

Unlike arbitration, mediation is not the adjudication of a conflict but an effort to reach agreement between parties using a neutral intermediary to facilitate and guide negotiations.

The primary advantage of mediation is that when parties resolve the conflict, they also control the outcome. If agreement can't be reached, the mediation process remains confidential and the parties proceed with courts, arbitration, or some other proceeding.

Mediation and arbitration and traditional litigation are not mutually exclusive, and are often complementary. Some State court systems require mediation prior to trial at the outset of a conflict resolution process or before the fact finding hearings. If no settlement is achieved, mediation can be employed at both stages. An advantage of mediation is that it narrows issues and results in a more efficient arbitration or judicial litigation process.

The Case for Arbitration and Mediation

If we agree that enterprise risk management includes a conflict resolution plan, I strongly recommend arbitration and mediation since virtually every transaction requires navigating legal systems, language, cultural customs and practices, monetary, and logistics challenges. Unlike judges and juries, arbitrators not only have the requisite experience and sophistication to resolve conflicts, they are chosen by both parties based on those attributes.

This approach can be particularly effective when companies work together to bring products and services to market. While some "partnerships" are formal, companies often work together in less structured purchaser/vendor relationships. Whatever the approach, they take time, energy and money and it can be difficult to replicate. Above all, it is critical that conflicts are resolved without destroying relationships. "Scorched earth" tactics of litigation and trial attorneys have costs far beyond the expense of litigation. Since trial attorneys don't focus on costs, executives and directors must. Arbitration avoids "scorched earth" tactics.

Meditation helps parties reach an agreement that both find acceptable, so there is no place for destructive "scorched earth" tactics. There is generally "give and take" and the relationship between parties is more likely to be preserved. In fact, it is not uncommon for parties to enter a new deal or expand an existing one.

Confidentiality

Business conflicts often involve confidential information – pricing, profitability, delivery schedules, formulas, or other trade secrets. Traditional courts have mechanisms and procedures to protect corporate trade secrets, but these forums and records are public. Judges must be convinced of the need for confidentiality, and even when documents are declared confidential, mistakes can happen.

The norm for arbitration is privacy and confidentiality. If the parties determine what can and cannot be disclosed about a conflict or its resolution, arbitration is the preferred path.

As mentioned earlier, in a world of social media and 24-hour news streams, there is a constant demand for titillating "news." Facts and context are often ignored and headlines are blasted out onto the wires and airwaves. The importance of confidentiality, and the ability to privately resolve conflicts, can't be overstated.

Speed

"Time is money" and it is rare when parties don't want a swift resolution of a conflict. Arbitrations are the preferred approach because they conclude quickly, appeals are swift, and judicial review is limited.

Reaching the Right Decision

Perhaps the most significant advantage is that arbitrators almost always have subject matter expertise. They are equipped to grasp the basics of the conflict, assign appropriate blame, and calculate damages. In other venues, you risk a run-away jury swayed by irrelevant matters or a judge that won't "get it".

Case Study – Toro Company

The Toro Company, a Minnesota manufacturer of lawn mowers and snow blowers, began addressing liability claims and customer complaints in the early 1990's. Andrew R. (Drew) Byers, Toro's Senior Manager of Corporate Product Integrity, led and implemented a three-step program to address the escalating costs and risks of customer litigation. Buyers explained, "We decided that we wanted to regain control of our money, of our documents, of our reputation and of our time."[1] "We haven't had a single corporate officer deposed in the last 11 years", Byers reported during a panel discussion in 2002[2]. A colleague at the same conference reported that after six years, "Toro's early intervention program has saved $50M."[3]

The three steps of Toro's program are prevention, early intervention/accident investigation, and pre-litigation mediation. The metrics speak for themselves:

- Before 1991, Toro's average litigation costs/fees were $47,252. Between 1992 and 2006, costs averaged $10,607, a 77% reduction[4].
- Before 1991, Toro's average per-claim verdicts/settlements were $68,368. Between 1992 and 2006, the average was $32,232, a 53% reduction[5].
- Before 1991, Toro's average total cost to close a file was $115,620. Between 1992 and 2006, the average was $42,839, a 63% reduction.[6]
- Before 1992, the average lifespan of a claim was 24 months. Between 1992 and 2006, the average was 9.8 months, a 59% reduction.[7]

Conclusion

Toro and other companies that have a conflict resolution strategy in place, offer strong arguments for early intervention by skilled mediators. Every conflict settled is one where both financial and reputational risks have been managed. When conflicts can't be settled, arbitration is usually the superior process to manage risk.

It is important to recognize that strategic and systemic conflict management programs do not only reduce risks, they sometimes prevent conflicts *altogether* because the programs themselves lead to a proactive, customer-centric review of products, processes and procedures – the key to building a positive reputation that results in solid financial results.

References

[1] "New Skills and Renewed Challenges Building Better Negotiation Skills; Dealing with the In-House Client"; ADR in Asia and Latin America, and More, 20 ALTHCL 137 (2002), p. 13

[2] *Id.*

[3] *Id.*

[4] "Toro's Alternative Conflict Resolution Program," slide 13, http://accord-adr.com/Articles.htm,

[5] *Id.* at slide 14

[6] *Id.* at slide 15

[7] *Id.* at slide 16

A Recipe for
Better Boardroom Leadership

Jeff Dodson
EVP, Strawn Arnold & Associates

Bio

Jeff Dodson is an Executive Vice President with Strawn Arnold &
Associates, Ltd., a retained life sciences executive recruiting firm.
Over his 15-year career in executive search, Jeff has recruited senior
executives and board members for clients in life sciences, consumer
products and non-profits. Prior to joining Strawn Arnold, Jeff held
leadership positions with two global executive recruiting firms as
Leader of the Americas pharmaceutical practice, Leader of the US
Life Science practice, and as the Chicago Office Leader. Prior to
entering executive search, Jeff was an executive with a multinational
consumer packaged goods company where he served as Vice President,
International Business Development; and, Managing Director, Middle
East and Africa. Jeff has been named one of the top 100 corporate

governance professionals in the U.S. by the National Association of Corporate Directors (NACD).

Key Points

- It takes more than deep knowledge of a company or an industry to be a valuable board leader.
- You must understand the culture as well as operating norms for a Board of Directors.
- Board leaders must invest time and energy into building relationships with individual board members to increase engagement and collaboration.

A Recipe for Better Boardroom Leadership

When you think about joining a Board, the price of entry is often relevant industry or leadership experience. But the effectiveness of a board is determined by far more than that, and includes the governance structure, operating model and culture of the board itself. A board, like any other organization, has its own personalities, challenges and rhythm. Understanding those nuances is critical for the success of a new leader.

A new Board Chair or Lead Director already has experience on the board and often rather clear ideas about how well the board is functioning and what changes might be helpful. As a collection of peers, a board depends on collaboration as well as patient, subtle influence by the leader. While this approach lengthens discussion and may delay some decisions, it also increases engagement and alignment.

Board governance requires robust systems, processes and awareness of relevant procedural best practices. Board *leadership*, on the other hand, is predicated on building relationships with individual board members and creating a culture where relationships among members are respectful and collegial. It is the relationship-side of the equation that demands a significant investment of time in and out of committee and full board meetings.

A typical board agenda for a public company or large non-profit organization might involve a board dinner the evening before, committee meetings the following morning, and a three to four hour full board meeting over a working lunch before members head for the airport. Unfortunately, regulatory "hygiene" consumes much of the agenda with the remaining time devoted to things a board is supposed to do – organizational strategy, management succession and enterprise risk mitigation.

With that schedule, how can CEOs, board chairs, or lead directors develop insightful, close relationships with board members? How do they gain perspective about committee operations, organizational strategy and the executive team? How can they identify potential problems that might be brewing within the board and resolve them so that members are aligned in good times and bad?

Board leaders must communicate with individual directors between board and committee meetings. This could mean regular phone calls to update members on initiatives; video conferences to discuss issues with one or more members of the board; invitations to join the leader in meetings with senior executives that a director may not typically get to know; or occasional visits if there are important issues to discuss or problems to resolve. Whatever the form, it is all about regular communication and engaging individual members in the company's future.

Board dynamics and governance practices vary. Boards of large, public multinationals are held to much different standards than those for family-owned, private equity or venture-backed companies. Large national or multinational non-profit organizations also need more sophisticated governance than small regional or local non-profits.

Here are eight things executives must understand to be more effective leaders in the boardroom:

1. **The enterprise.** Is it a public company, a PE/venture backed company, or a large, visible non-profit organization? Large public companies will generally operate with perceived best practices regarding board processes, board composition,

director independence, etc. Private equity and venture-backed companies often have investor representatives on their boards with different objectives, valuation perspectives and investment horizons.

2. **The state of the enterprise.** Is the organization challenged with rapid growth or in need of restructuring and a turnaround? Is the industry strong or crippled by disruptive and competitive changes? Will you be involved in incremental, evolutionary changes in strategy and operating practices or something more dramatic?

3. **Board composition.** Do you have the right people around the table? Do they have the expertise, company/industry knowledge and perspective needed to lead a company through business and organizational challenges? Are current board members the best ones to be at the helm in the future?

4. **Board culture.** Before you can change a culture, you must first understand the culture you have. How are key decisions made? Are they discussed and debated at the board dinner the night before, in committee meetings, in sessions of the full board, or in hallway conversations between certain individuals between meetings? Are some voices "louder" than others because of strong personalities, weakness of other directors, the power from a strong committee leader or someone with a large ownership position? In other words, do certain members have disproportionate influence and power, and how will you resolve that issue?

   Are all directors participating fully? If not, why not? Do they lack expertise? Are they "over-boarded" and unable to spend sufficient time on meeting preparation? Is the board culture one that includes candid feedback and constructive confrontation, or a scripted, passive aggressive dynamic with tough conversations held off-line?

5. **The strategy for building director engagement and relationships.** It is important for new board leaders to *plan* the formal and informal processes they will use to drive cultural

change. "I'll get to it when I can," isn't a strategy – and many CEOs who didn't take the time to build relationships found themselves without board support when they needed it most.

6. **Understanding unspoken realities and broader context.** Not all companies (especially large public multinationals) bow to the god of shareholder capitalism – an assumption that Americans and Anglos are particularly prone to make. Large public companies in Europe, Asia and Latin America are often viewed as "national champions" and are expected to weigh the interests of other stakeholders, e.g. communities, organized labor, domestic politicians, and strategic national interests, as much as shareholders. As the leader of one of these companies, you ignore this unspoken norm at your peril. CEOs and non-executive chairman regularly lose their jobs over this issue.

7. **Governance and fiduciary oversight vs. operations.** There are different views about what constitutes the board's fiduciary oversight depending on whether it is a public or private company. One person's "reasonable and proper" may be another's "interference". Members of the executive leadership team and the board need to talk about this issue and define general boundaries. If the board dynamic isn't working, or if the board persists in focusing on operational matters, the chair and the CEO can work together to make changes. PE/ Venture firms or other private enterprises often have different standards and board members are often much more involved in operations.

8. **The challenge of large boards.** A board that is too small may deprive the organization of important perspectives and skill sets and can interfere with an appropriate committee structure. A board that is too large may become so focused on process and consensus that little gets done. Tough, "bet the company" decisions are all but impossible to make in a tight timeframe and as a result, events can overtake the company.

Conclusion

Leading a board is analogous to being a player/coach on a sports team. To unleash the power of a group of capable people, the leader establishes the game plan, sorts out the best position for each player, and then creates an environment that allows that to happen.

And there is one other thing to remember from your days in youth league sports: no player is indispensable.

Section 3

Unleashing Potential

Linking Culture and Strategy

Michael A. Pulick, Jr
Advisor, Warberg Pincus LLC

Bio

Michael Pulick served as President of Grainger's International and U.S. businesses from 2008-2013. He joined Grainger in 1999 and held a number of roles with increased responsibility in the company's customer service and product management areas. Prior to joining Grainger, he was in management roles at General Electric from 1986 to 1999. Mr. Pulick holds a BS in Electrical Engineering from Michigan Technological University and a MBA from the University of Chicago. He has served as an adjunct professor at Lake Forest Graduate School of Management, a member of Illinois Institute of Technology's Board of Trustees, and board member of Junior Achievement of Chicago.

> *"A great strategy alone won't win a game or a battle; the win comes from basic blocking and tackling." Built to Last*

When describing a company's culture, I often say, "It's the way things get done around here". In other words, it's the basic blocking and tackling. A great strategy is not enough to be successful; the key to winning is linking culture and strategy.

Key Points

- Build a culture that can deliver, and your strategy will thrive.
- Strategy – everyone has to live it.
- Simplify your strategy – a great narrative is clear, concise, and compelling.
- To win, culture and strategy must be linked.

What You Need To Know

Build a culture that can deliver and your strategy will thrive. When I began leading the largest division of an $8 billion Fortune 500 company, I was in a position for the first time where I felt I could have a real impact on the way we went to market and our strategy to win.

The company, founded in 1927, was led by the founder and his son for the first 70 years and the culture had been decidedly paternalistic. We treated people very well, and all had great respect for authority, and deferred to the leader above us.

In my first meeting with our top 200 leaders, I wanted to tell them how I thought we were doing, so I issued a report card. Although some marks were higher, I gave us a C+ for culture. Why? We were slow and bureaucratic, we had lots of meetings, we made decisions by consensus, we had a low risk tolerance, we were too comfortable with the status quo, we had created an environment that lacked transparency and encouraged passive-aggressive behavior, e.g., saying one thing in a meeting and doing something else out of the room, and, we weren't customer focused; we made decisions thinking about ourselves first, and our customers second.

So, there I was, a new leader in a paternalistic culture, and I'd just told my team that I wasn't pleased with the way we were behaving. The silence was deafening. As the shock began to wear off, I encouraged them to think about why culture was important. Finally the team realized that the current culture could not deliver on our strategy.

Strategy – everyone has to live it. We began by building a clear strategy built on helping our customers save time and money. It was important to involve leaders in creating the strategy, rather than just presenting it as a done deal since execution is all about buy-in and accountability for outcomes. We developed a one-page strategic framework built on three pillars and tied everything that happened in the business to these pillars.

To begin shifting culture, we completely transformed the way that we conducted meetings – especially with our top 200 leaders. Meetings moved from telling/presenting, to sharing knowledge of the leaders in the room. We minimized the use of PowerPoint and began to rely on more organic ways of communicating. We organized small Action Learning Teams to generate dialogue and to build cross-functional relationships. We gave them assignments to be completed between meetings to create continuity.

Simplify your strategy – a great narrative is clear, concise, and compelling. To help sharpen and simplify our strategy, the senior leadership team developed a story that explained what our strategy was, and why and how it would work. Our intention was to find a better way to communicate the strategy to all 13,000 team members so that everyone understood what we were trying to achieve. Instead of clicking through endless slides, we challenged ourselves to draw pictures to represent our parts of the story. The result was a set of stick figures that were easy to draw and easy to remember. It was more compelling and people paid attention.

At our next top 200-leader meeting, we formed teams and asked each one to create a five-minute skit describing the specific things that team members could do to improve our culture and enable our strategy.

The winning team's idea was to get every team member to walk a mile in our customers' shoes.

The team "won" a yearlong project to implement their idea, and while some wished they could have gotten the second place Starbuck's gift cards, the project was extremely successful. It resulted in naming conference rooms for customers, an internally accessible database of customer stories, and a company-wide practice of starting all meetings with a customer story to keep our focus where it belonged.

At the same meeting we presented the newly created strategic narrative. It was enthusiastically received, especially accompanied by simple hand-drawn pictures. The strategic story was told in about 40 minutes, and after a brief Q and A, I asked for a volunteer to come up and repeat it. One of our sales leaders came to the stage and told the story perfectly in about two minutes, including drawing all the pictures. She received a standing ovation. We knew then that we had something powerful: a memorable and repeatable story that was concise and clear, and that would make people think differently about our strategic goal.

To win, culture and strategy must be linked. When we disseminated our strategic narrative to the entire organization, people in the business were inspired to think about our customers more often and in new and different ways. If you walked through one of our facilities, you'd likely see the narrative hand-drawn on a white board or printed on a mouse pad, or be greeted by life-size customer cardboard cutouts. At sales meetings, you might be asked to apply a temporary tattoo of the stick-figure drawings, a symbol of putting our customers first. A group of team members even created a rap song and video that used content of the narrative for lyrics.

These were not corporate mandated promotions of the strategy. The strength of the approach was that Team members created them all. The power of communicating a strategy that's concise, memorable and repeatable is that everyone hears it in his or her own way and understands it from that perspective. This helps people in the business "own" it and by building ownership, you unleash the creativity of your organization.

Conclusion

When you follow these few basic principles, you will learn that your strategy will take on a life of its own and won't depend on leaders to drive it.

I've learned that strategy alone is not a competitive advantage. Culture is the blocking and tackling that ensures successful execution. Linking culture *and* strategy is a great way to win.

Embracing Change

Steve Ritter

Founder & CEO, The Teamclock Institute

Bio

Steve Ritter has served as a human resources leader, teacher, author, and consultant. He is a fellow of the American College of Healthcare Executives, the Founder and CEO of the Team Clock Institute, and the Managing Director of the Midwest Institute & Center for Workplace Innovation. Steve is on the faculty of the Center for Professional Excellence at Elmhurst College. He is the former Senior Vice President and Director of Human Resources at Leaders Bank, named #1 Best Place to Work in Illinois in 2006, AHA Heart Healthy Workplace Platinum Award winner in 2009, and winner of the American Psychological Association's Psychologically Healthy Workplace Award in 2010.

Key Points

A fundamental principle is that organizational change is a cyclical process:

- **Invest**: continuously calibrate norms and goals to accommodate new realities.
- **Trust**: Embrace diversity in decision making and non-negotiable accountability for results.
- **Innovate**: Leverage healthy conflict and differences to drive innovation and smart risk taking.
- **Distance**: Expect mature, resilient responses during change.
- **Evolve**: Recognize the cyclical nature of the change process.

What You Need to Know

All living things have predictable cycles of evolution, and organizations, businesses and markets are no different. Awareness of where you are on the cycle helps move the organization in the right direction. Where are we? What got us here? What do we need to do next? This shared awareness is the platform for effective teamwork in the midst of change. Leaders who acknowledge, interpret, and embrace change as the lifeblood of the business will build commitment and engagement in the organization.

Invest

It's important to define why a business exists, its mission, and the values that define how the team will deliver on that mission. Although "vision" appears to have many different definitions, mine is simple: our overarching goal. These combined elements define the "way we do business" and shape rules, roles, boundaries, and expectations.

These elements evolve over time with changes in leadership, talent, market conditions, and competitive landscapes. Any significant change provides an opportunity to recalibrate team expectations and behavior, and to reaffirm a leader's philosophy, mission, values, and vision. In some cases, little change is required. In others, it might create circumstances where more substantive change is needed.

Change is a fleeting window of opportunity to validate team direction. Do you embrace constructive conflict to enable creative tension? Do you invite diverse perspectives to support innovation? What defines your "way?" Is the team still aligned with the vision?

Trust

Trust in the workplace is both earned and eroded every day. Accountability is key to every interaction. Just as strategy without execution is meaningless, mutual accountability and follow-through builds trust, and pointing fingers and avoiding accountability fractures it.

There are many benefits of building cultures based on trust and accountability. In the short term, they allow teams to connect and collaborate – and that sense of collaboration is obvious to others. Over the long term, trust serves as a safety net. As your own experience shows, we are far more willing to lean on a colleague we trust during times of significant change.

Innovate

Corporate leaders see an ever-expanding gap between the capacity of the current workforce and the complexity of the work. Innovation based on cross-functional collaboration can help bridge that gap. As organizations open up to new ideas and approaches, leaders often find that it unleashes creativity among diverse team members, helps people grow, and equips people to take smart risks. In many cases, this approach results in a new solution to an old problem.

Once team members begin to trust each other, they can explore new ideas with genuine curiosity and a sense of adventure. Rather than shooting down other people's ideas, they will learn to build on other points of view. Some ideas will be good ones; others won't. Companies known for innovation recognize that small failures can lead to significant innovations.

Distance

It is difficult to move away from the status quo. As leaders, we have a stake in certain products, services, or approaches to the market. Letting go requires you to have trust and confidence that the new idea is a better one. It's a bit like parenting. You have to provide context and tools, trust in what you've taught them, and give them the autonomy they need to demonstrate their ability. This is how talent is nurtured and succession candidates are identified.

Most of us cope well under normal circumstances, but stress can bring out the worst in us. As a CEO, it is your job to maintain focus and calm in the midst of a major change or crisis since the eyes and ears of all constituents are focused on you. You might need to step away to re-group, but step back in with energy and quiet confidence to reassure everyone that things are under good control.

Evolve

All problems have two phases: challenge and opportunity. In the challenge phase, the objective is to define the problem. In the opportunity phase, the goal is to decide what actions to take to move forward. Some leaders spend more time diagnosing than solving; others, assess the problem quickly and dive right in to action steps. Both approaches work, but the objective must be timely, thoughtful movement.

Change requires us to see, adapt and refocus which can be particularly difficult if you are exhausted from a prolonged change process. It's counterintuitive to reinvest in something that has been an emotional drain. But, reinvestment refuels the system, forces growth, and renews the cycle.

Conclusion

Teams confront numerous rounds of change in the life cycle of any healthy organization. At each point, individual team members must decide whether they are "in or out". Most organizations have some people who embrace change and want to keep their foot on the accelerator; and others who want to keep their foot on the brake to protect life as they know it. Creating the right balance determines the pace at which an organization can adapt to change.

As the CEO, it will be important to ensure that your team has the following things in common: a shared vision; diversity of thought; mutual respect; trust; the ability to innovate by taking smart risks;

the ability to adapt quickly to change and reinvest in the new reality; mutual accountability and openness to change.

Suggested Reading

Team Clock: *A Guide to Breakthrough Teams,* Steve Ritter

Transforming Companies

Joe Lawler

Operating Partner, Kohlberg & Company

Bio

Joe has had a 30-year career in top leadership and board roles including President, CEO, and Board Chair for ModusLink Global Solutions, a global reverse logistics company; EVP of RR Donnelley, an $8B global print management and logistics company; and EVP of CML Group, a specialty consumer products company. Prior to these roles he co-founded Lawler Botsford and Co., a private equity and operating management firm; and held senior positions with Fingerhut Companies and Gander Mountain where he also served on the Board. He currently serves on the Boards of Allagash Brewing Company, AFN Logistics, LLC; PPC Industries, Inc.; and Dicom Transportation Group, Inc. He is also a Senior Board Advisor for Kohlberg & Company, a leading middle-market private equity firm.

Key Points

- You can't begin to fix a company until you know what's broken.
- Successful turnarounds are built upon a healthy culture and agreed upon values that permeate the organization.
- Putting the right people in the right roles, doing the right thing, takes more time than you might think.

Background

Turning around a company is as "simple" as figuring out what's broken. Most CEOs who walk into new roles have done their homework. They've interviewed members of the board and the management team and have reviewed information that is publicly available. They arrive with educated guesses about what the organization needs. But, CEOs quickly learn that what they thought they understood isn't the reality. Within a few short months, or weeks, they are buried in financial projections; sales pipelines; key customer reviews; market analysis; merchandising; marketing; supply chain; and all other facets of the business. And the final analysis is often worse than they thought.

But there are real advantages of coming into a company from outside. You are more objective about the business and the senior team, you recognize no sacred cows (but be sure to confirm that with your board), and you have no single person or strategy that you must support. You can see the opportunities and challenges more clearly and use your own experience and industry best practices as benchmarks for the organization. You can also begin to assess whether the existing management team can deliver.

A three-part strategy. I've learned that a solid strategy has three parts. The first is a vision for the company's future—where are we going and how? Second, clear quantifiable 3-5 year goals supported by annual objectives tied directly to the budget; and third, a set of strategic initiatives that represent the programs to be implemented in the current year.

Culture and values. Another critical element of a successful turnaround is to figure out existing culture and values. It is very hard to fix/build any company – particularly one that extends across multiple locations, geographies, and experiences – if there are no agreed upon values that ALL employees can embrace. Values need to be clear and easy to remember, but they must hold deep meaning if you are going to engage the hearts and minds of your team. For example, you might hold "integrity" as an important value, but we all know that the term is defined differently in different cultures as evidenced by the Foreign Corrupt Practices Act. The bottom line is this: Exceptional corporate cultures can be created with a highly diverse team that shares and embraces common values.

Organizational design. Once you have determined the "what" and "how" parts of the puzzle, it will be time to focus on the "who". Structuring the team and the organization to deliver on the strategy becomes clearer once you understand the qualities and competencies you need to execute. Having said that, it isn't easy. Make sure you have the right people at the strategy table. Work closely with them to define the backgrounds and experience that will be required and the reward system that will support high performers. At this point, you make sure they focus on the right things, things according to the values that have been agreed upon, and get out of the way (most but not all of the time).

Conclusion

Culture, Strategy and Structure are the three interconnected disciplines that have helped me lead in a wide range of businesses over the past thirty years and still provides a framework for the Board and Advisory work I'm involved in today.

Suggested Readings

The Art of War, Sun Tzu

Atlas Shrugged, Ayn Rand

Competitive Strategy, Michael Porter

Good to Great, Jim Collins

Above the Line, Jim Dethmer

A Path to Transformation

Mike Suchsland
Principal, Joplin Consulting

Bio

Mike Suchsland is a seasoned business, division, and portfolio President. He has a history of driving value through business creation, organization transformation, and cultural turnaround. Mike most recently led a $3B global software, services, and information division of Thomson Reuters with over 10,000 employees. In that role he quickly moved to build a new strategy, made tough decisions to realign the organization, focused investments, and drove innovation, growth, and profitability. Mike enjoys metagrobology and is happy to explain what that is over a cocktail.

Background

Leading change as a new CEO is fraught with potential missteps. You must learn how to recognize and overcome passive resistance, motivate dispirited employees, and avoid wasting organizational energy and political capital.

What You Need to Know

As a new CEO, my first attempt at transformation appeared simple. I seemingly knew exactly what to do, how to do it, and believed I could just share my wisdom with the organization and it would happen. So, what did I do? I hosted an all-employee meeting and sent out a bunch of memos.

Guess what? I failed miserably. A rigid, imbedded, and invisible culture raised a defensive shield to block my efforts. The more energy I expended, the stronger the resistance became. Something had to change, and I realized that "something" was me.

Fortunately, I realized I had failed to take the most important first step: to explain why change was necessary and ask for help from the organization to address the challenge. When I did, employees began to raise their hands to support change, working groups formed, and decisions were made and implemented. Over time, a positive sense of community emerged as my colleagues rallied around the new vision.

Lessons Learned

You must clearly explain what change is needed and why.

You have a change agenda. Your challenge is to share that agenda by explaining what's needed and why, in simple, straightforward terms. Describe a picture of what kind of business employees can look forward to and how that differs from today. Employees are smart and resilient—you can share your vision of a successful future, challenges and all, and they will rally.

Be specific. In one case it was easy for me to say, "We can no longer make decisions in organizational silos. We have to work together across functions." But how do you make that happen? The heavy lifting was putting together 3, 12, and 36 month change management goals that were practical and achievable. We published those goals and regularly updated employees broadly on our progress. This high level of transparency reassured employees that we were on the right track and built trust in the management team.

Invite discussion and debate about the change agenda.

When I was younger, I thought that a CEO was an all-powerful character who could dictate an agenda and have employees respond. In today's large, dispersed organizations, command and control structures don't drive behavior change. I realized that *my* vision must become *our* vision to make everyone part of the solution. I issued a clear invitation to all employees asking for input, was open to feedback, and willing to use their ideas to improve the end product.

This approach set the stage for giving employees a real voice in the future of the organization. It is as simple as describing the proposed vision and asking "What do you think?" Encourage them to talk to their colleagues, make suggestions, and send you that information so that it can help create the strongest plan.

Employees with "skin in the game" may still have concerns, but they will better understand why change is necessary and what they can do to support it. Healthy, open debate helps drive alignment, and the opportunity to voice an opinion builds acceptance and support for the future.

Have honest conversations.

Change is *personal*. As a leader, I encouraged my senior team to "walk the walls" and "cover the cubes." This was sometimes as simple as approaching an employee and asking the question "What are you working on?" and "How can I help?" These touch points began to build trust and establish my reputation as a leader willing to weigh different opinions.

I learned all this the hard way. We once delivered an annual software update to customers so advanced that their computers couldn't run it. After a lot of internal hand wringing, we spent millions buying new computers for customers so they could use our products. Later, when

I asked our technology developers what the heck had happened, the response was very simple: "We could have predicted this, but no one bothered to ask us." Shame on us.

Recognize that some employees just aren't comfortable voicing their opinions publicly, so you need to make it easy for them to send a note directly and in confidence. Let them know you received it and promise to follow up if appropriate. Actions like this build trust and commitment.

Use internal social media effectively and transparently.

Organizations use confidential social media platforms to host employee conversations on topics of mutual business interest. Those platforms serve an important need by tying together geographically and functionally diverse employees.

In discussions where employees are debating the future, you should offer your unique insight or contribution. This reassures employees that you are actively listening and responding to their ideas.

Transparency and truthfulness drive the quality of discussion. Be honest. If layoffs are expected, say so. If a re-organization is likely, say so. You probably won't know exactly what is going to happen, but tell them that too, along with a promise to share information as it becomes available.

You will have the final say, but will be far better informed because employees have shared their thoughts and suggestions with you. As a result, implementation will be smoother and more enthusiastic because you have brought them into the decision making process.

Revise the final plan based on employee feedback.

You have an original vision, robust feedback from employees, and an opportunity to build rapport that extends deeply into the organization.

The revised vision with emphasis on the changes that were made based on employee feedback is a powerful thing. It's no longer your vision; it's the *collective* vision with far broader buy-in, acceptance, and support.

At every step along the way, you convey your burning desire to see the organization succeed. Now debate stops and employees must respond with their own passion for transformation through effective implementation. Alignment is high, and action will now be fast, deep, and aggressive.

Enable support for implementation.

You can't impose action plans from the top. You can certainly describe *what* needs to be done, but those on the ground must determine *how* it should be done. Employee-led teams ensure the most deeply embedded and lasting change.

During one transformation, I created middle-management teams to develop ideas around cultural innovation and new product development. Individuals on these teams continued to report to their manager for their "day job", but were accountable to me for ideas to transform the culture. They were motivated by having direct access to me and a voice in where the organization was going. And I heard things directly rather than having them filtered by several layers of management. We adopted several of their recommendations, and reassigned some to serve as leaders of those initiatives.

The overall process had one more benefit. It gave me an unprecedented window into organizational talent. I got to know colleagues who could think more broadly, who were enthusiastic about the future, and who were willing to engage. These people were our future leaders who would create change, rally other employees, and lead the business of the future.

These six steps to organizational transformation are fueled by truth-telling and powered by transparency. When you lead with honesty, purpose and passion, change will become culturally embedded and self-sustaining, and will create a legacy far beyond your tenure.

Recommended Reading

- **The First 90 Days:** *Proven Strategies for Getting Up to Speed Faster and Smarter*, Michael D. Watkins
- **From Values to Action:** *The Four Principles of Values-Based Leadership*, Harry M. Kraemer
- **Leading Out Loud:** *Inspiring Change Through Authentic Communication*, Terry Pearce

Decision Rights

Jeff Bennett
Founder and Managing Partner
Amphora Consulting

Bio

Jeff Bennett founded Amphora Consulting in 2003 and is currently the Managing Partner. Amphora collaborates closely with its clients to embed key principles of business strategy, and to develop and execute winning growth initiatives. Prior to founding the firm he was a Partner at Booz, Allen and Hamilton where he led high-level organizational transformations in agricultural, industrial, distribution and packaged goods companies. He is a recognized thought leader in the use of decision rights to drive organizational change, and has been published in *Leader to Leader*, *Strategy & Business* and *Harvard Business Review*.

Key Points

- Decision Rights transforms organizations. It delegates critical business decisions to those in the organization who possess real time information.
- Your job is to provide the necessary perspective and appropriate incentives so that they make decisions in the company's best interest.
- Create organization structure and processes to support, empower, and improve decisions over time.
- Done correctly, the model can lead to rapid and dramatic improvement in performance, a more energized workforce, and a resilient, self-correcting company.

What You Need to Know

Decision Rights is a unique approach to organizational transformation that drives critical business decisions deep into the organization to individuals who have the best, most timely information; the necessary information and perspective; and the appropriate incentives to make decisions in the company's best interest.

This approach replaces "lines and boxes" organizational design and outperforms them. Incentives for decision-makers are front and center in this model because it is based on what motivates people. This approach is particularly effective in functional areas that require creativity and flexibility, e.g., sales and R&D. Motivation is critical in these roles and traditional 'command and control' models come up short.

The theory of decision rights is grounded in a relatively obscure field known as 'economics of organizations.' The basic premise is that the laws of economics don't stop at the firm level. Individuals continue to evaluate trade-offs as they weigh how to spend their time and resources. Key principles are:

- A bias toward de-centralization. Decision making is delegated to the *lowest* appropriate level where specific, timely information resides – unless there is a *compelling* reason to make it elsewhere.

- It shifts the model from central planning staffs and powerful budget officers to market-style processes. It allocates scarce resources to individuals/departments based on risk and reward, e.g., to a division that bids the highest on a day of sales-force time.
- It creates an organization-wide focus on those few things that require scale or technical expertise, and eliminates activities that can be bought more cheaply from others.
- Accountability is part of everyone's job description to ensure that people at all levels experience the consequences – positive and negative – of their own decisions.
- Decision rights establish a few unambiguous values that everyone understands, that leaders uphold, and that anchor decisions to clear values.

This common sense model defines a new role for leaders. While some can make the shift; others can't. Some CEOs think of themselves as all-knowing, tough, take-charge types who must centralize authority and make all important capital allocation decisions themselves. (Larry Ellison, the CEO of Oracle, is said to review all decisions involving sums above $50,000). They structure organizations as if only a single superstar is needed for success.

Companies that adopt a decision rights model have found that decentralized leadership works in the short and long run. Their executives resist media-fueled, "strong hand at the helm" behavior, recognizing that their personal credibility would be irrevocably damaged if they reverted to a command and control model. They also use incentives to link purpose to outcomes, and recognize that values and behaviors can be cultivated, but not controlled. This creates organizations with the capacity to self-govern and adapt based on successes and failures.

There is no doubt that leaders have to exercise restraint when times are tough and Boards and shareholders demand action. It is an ongoing challenge to relinquish control and trust that people will make the right decisions and do the right thing. But, that discipline ultimately proves the success of the model.

Conclusion

Decision Rights represents a powerful way to think about organizational transformation. Done correctly, it can lead to rapid and dramatic performance improvement, a more energized workforce, and a resilient, self-correcting company. Although navigating this change isn't easy, it is successful.

Additional Reading

"Constrained Change–Unconstrained Results", Jeffrey Bennett, *Strategy and Business*, 1998

"The Organization vs. The Strategy–Solving the Alignment Paradox", Jeffrey Bennett, Thomas Pernsteiner, Paul Kucourek, Steve Hedlund, *Strategy and Business*, 2001

Are You *Relevant* to Your Customers?

Gary Mitchiner
Co-Founder, *The Growth Leaders LLC*

Bio

Gary Mitchiner is the co-founder of The Growth Leaders LLC, a client-centric business development coaching firm. Previously, he held marketing leadership roles in advertising agencies and client-side marketing groups and contributed to the growth of Hyatt Hotels, Citi Group, McDonalds, Nuveen Investments, AON Hewitt, Deloitte, Mesirow Financial, Baker & McKenzie and CVS Health. He is a certified performance coach with 25 years of post-graduate education with The Newfield Group, The Aji Network, The Institute for Generative Leadership, and the Harvard School of Business Executive Leadership Program. He's a University of Missouri graduate with a degree in client-centric communication.

Key Points

- Business growth comes from being increasingly relevant to customers.
- The Plot Mountain listening tool and practice is a Top 1% performance skill used to establish, regain and sustain your company's relevance to customers.
- The tool is easy-to-learn and will give you a competitive advantage.

What You Need to Know

Your organization can become irrelevant to customers faster now than any time in history. Rapid shifts in customer needs and a constant stream of new offers from new competitors are an ongoing threat. Keeping your company *relevant* is the key to growth.

What I've learned

The first thing I've learned is that the "build it and customers will come" business model is history. Today, it's about listening for the story (results) the customer wants to achieve ("we want to double sales in five years") and making yourself relevant to that outcome. The second thing I've learned is that customers notice and appreciate it when you pay attention to them and ask about their growth story, and will prefer you to your competitors as a result.

All businesses must focus on what customers care about, and build products and services to match. Many leadership teams have focused internally for so long that this is 180-degree shift to focus on the customer is a significant challenge. The plot mountain story listening tool will help.

Plot mountain story listening tool & practice

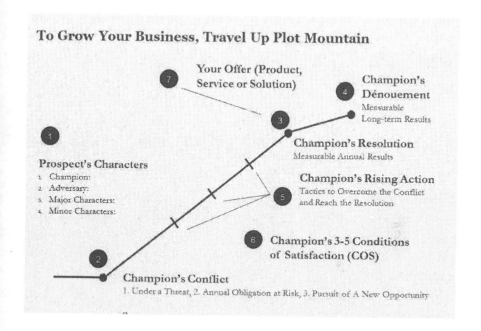

To Grow Your Business, Travel Up Plot Mountain

7 — Your Offer (Product, Service or Solution)

4 — Champion's Dénouement
Measurable Long-term Results

3

Champion's Resolution
Measurable Annual Results

1

Prospect's Characters
1. Champion:
2. Adversary:
3. Major Characters:
4. Minor Characters:

Champion's Rising Action
Tactics to Overcome the Conflict
and Reach the Resolution

5

6 — Champion's 3-5 Conditions
of Satisfaction (COS)

2

Champion's Conflict
1. Under a Threat, 2. Annual Obligation at Risk, 3. Pursuit of A New Opportunity

Plot Mountain includes seven elements. Your offer to a prospect is dead *last* on that list.

First you must learn the first six elements of a prospect's story. Most of us haven't used this approach. In fact, we usually listen just long enough to find a way to "pitch" our product or service. This model flips the process to 2/3 listening and 1/3 talking—and in that order. Below you will find the seven simple elements of Plot Mountain and what to listen for in each. Although this approach is unfamiliar to you now, if you imagine any story, you will soon understand it.

1. The characters.

Every customer has a story. Every story has characters. You need to sort out who you are listening to and whether that person is the decision maker and accountable for results your product or service can help generate.

The champion: This person is responsible for annual and long term business results and the *denouement* (higher meaning) of accomplishing the annual results.

The adversary: The Champion views this person(s) as working against them. They can be internal or external. (It really *is* a person, by the way, not an issue or an economic threat.) All dramas, from Shakespeare to today, have a champion and an adversary because it's that tension that we find interesting. Steve Jobs' first internal adversaries were his board members. His second was his CEO, John Scully. His external adversary was Bill Gates.

Major players: These are the people the Champion counts on to work through conflicts, reach resolution/annual results, and achieve the *denouement* (higher meaning). You may not have direct access to the Champion, but your primary contact *can* and *will* share the Champion's story.

Minor players: There are always one or more minor players, but if your only contact is a minor player, you have a problem. Show that person respect but understand that it will be difficult for you to play a major role in the Champion's story if your only connection is to minor players.

Action Step: Think about a specific prospect you are pursuing. These same characters exist in that organization. Who is playing each role?

2. The conflict.

A story is always based on the Champion's conflict and conflict reveals itself in three levels. The first is a threat against the Champion – a real crisis – that can't be ignored. In the case of Johnson and Johnson, the Chairman/Champion had to find the person who put poison in bottles of Tylenol. The second level of conflict is when the Champion has made a commitment and believes that commitment is at risk. It's not a high level threat, but it is a very real concern. The third type of conflict is a new opportunity that the Champion wants to pursue. The conflict is created because when you pursue something new, you ignore other things. Steve Jobs used third level conflicts as his management style to drive new opportunities and products.

Action Step: There's a 99% chance that the Champion at your prospect company has a conflict. Try to find out what it is.

3. The resolution/annual result.

Resolution means just that: The Champion has overcome the conflict and achieved a measurable business result. An easy example is meeting an annual sales goal or achieving the annual operating margin.

Action Step: The Champion is focused on a specific result/resolution. See if you can learn what it is.

4. The *Denouement* (higher meaning from achieving the resolution).

Denouement means the final part of a play, movie, or narrative in which all of the strands of the plot are drawn together and all of your questions are answered.

Action Step: The Champion's story includes denouement but it is rarely discussed or shared. You need to build trust to draw it out. Once you do, you will have invaluable insight into the Champion's motivation and behavior.

5. Conditions of satisfaction/COS.

Conditions of Satisfaction are the 3-5 criteria that the Champion will use to gauge success. A Champion who is proactive will openly communicate these criteria to inside and outside resources to create a road-map to success. Criteria might include budget, timing, speed, quality standards, compatibility with current commitments and ethics. Champions will sometimes say, "We don't just want the results, we want to achieve the results in the *right* way."

Action Step: Once you learn the Champion's Conditions of Satisfaction, you can position your offer to match them.

6. The rising action (Tactics).

When you look at the Plot Mountain chart, this element is reflected in the vertical, angled line. Tactics are the actions to be taken to overcome conflict and reach resolution. Listen for the tactics that the Champion is using or considering. They may or may not include what you have to offer.

Action step: When you identify tactics, you need to know whether some other company has already filled the need that your firm was considering. Even so, those people may not be meeting the COS. If they are over budget and have missed deadlines, for example, you could have an opening wide enough to jump through.

7. Your offer of help.

Now and *only now*, are you in a position to make an offer. You have uncovered the six elements of the Champion's story, and you can now position your product or service offer as a relevant and perhaps essential way for them to fulfill their story.

Action step: Your listening has put you in a uniquely powerful position. You will be viewed as a relevant, highly differentiated resource who understands and empathizes with the Champion's story and the results he/she is trying to achieve.

Conclusion

Although Plot Mountain is unfamiliar, it isn't difficult. It just takes a little practice. Use a current customer situation and work through these steps. Drop in a few names in that prospect company and the pieces of intelligence you have already gathered. When you put it all in story form, you'll find that you have insights you wouldn't have developed any other way. You may also find some gaps in the story that need a bit more listening to uncover. In short, use this tool to differentiate your business in the eyes of potential clients by being relevant to their concerns. It will take your business growth to an entirely new level.

Cultivating Culture

Ron Hodge
Former Partner, Booz Allen Hamilton

Bio

Ron Hodge is a business leader with over 30 years of professional consulting experience. As a Senior Vice President/Partner at $5B management consulting firms, he championed "intrapreneurship," successfully leading start-up businesses and driving rapid growth and diversification of new lines of business, service offerings and key market segments. He was named the firm's Technology Practice Leader based on his reputation as a trusted advisor and expert in business performance and technology. Ron is currently working on his Ph.D., and serves on the board for business and educational institutions.

Key Points

- Organizational cultures change – and they should.
- It is important to align strategy, financial goals and culture.
- Identify and celebrate "Culture Stewards" in your organization.

- Anticipate and plan for cultural "tipping points".

Background

"Our culture has changed. *We've* changed. This just isn't the same place anymore."

I can't tell you how many times I have heard that from concerned colleagues. But the truth is, cultures are not static, nor should they be. They need new elements to enrich the environment and foster productivity and innovation. Even *good* cultures may need to exorcise bad elements. And bad cultures may need a complete change of leadership to resolve problems.

My firm's culture changed from when I started – it got much better. We embraced diversity programs, began to recognize and reward employees, and added incentives to promote collaboration rather than competition. Over time the change was graceful, incremental, and smooth.

The recipe for a "good to great" culture is more like a cake than a salad. In a salad, you combine ingredients but they remain discernible and unique. In a cake, ingredients are transformed so that none are easily identifiable. It's the magic of chemistry.

Some refer to their culture as part of their "secret sauce" – an intangible that creates unique value. But there is really no secret to it. Culture represents the people of the organization, their shared mission and aspirations, and their ability to work together. Strong cultures have leaders who share a vision, communicate well throughout change, and align strategy, finance and cultural values. The chemistry is strong – call it a "culture cake". Weak or dysfunctional cultures are fragmented, have no shared vision, lack communication, and are not aligned – more like a culture "salad".

Here are a few considerations that are critical to fostering strong cultures.

Strategic, financial and cultural alignment. In good times – high growth, high profits – alignment is pretty easy. In more challenging times, cultural norms veer off in different directions. Industry is littered with companies that needed to change strategic direction because of a change in ownership or poor financial results. Some have done it better than others.

Consulting firms often hire leaders from different industries who can take organizations down very different paths. For example, aerospace companies rely on large scale, high volume sales, generally at a lower margin. Consulting firms typically look to high margin plays and often don't target large-scale volume buys. There is no right or wrong. Each model requires different leaders, talent, and financial constructs to be successful, and each affects culture in terms of the talent hired, their aspirations, and their measures of success.

Culture stewards and communications. Many people "job hop" to stretch themselves with new challenges, opportunities, and environments. That churn can bring energy, ideas, and a new dynamic to your environment. But, every organization also needs a set of leaders that establish the tone, chart the course, and focus their attention on the long term. These people have the perspective of time – they know where the organization has been, and where it's going. They view changes in the context of a journey.

Identifying "culture stewards" and providing platforms to allow them to share context and perspective is essential to aligning culture. The "Steward in Chief" is the CEO whose message sets the tone for stockholders and the employees. Be it evolution or revolution, the spirit, vision and commitment of top leaders is the catalyst for cultural change.

Cultural tipping point. Mergers and acquisitions throw different cultures together. Even if both cultures are "good", they are likely quite different which makes assimilation and integration challenging. Unless they operate independently, those conflicts often diminish the value of the merger. I have served on the board of an organization that merged or acquired many other organizations. The diligence performed on candidate organizations included strategic, financial, and cultural fit.

Organic growth generated by internal resources often permits a graceful, evolutionary approach to cultural change. Yet some firms aggressively hire outside talent to infuse new ways of doing business without factoring in the new leader's commitment to change. It leads to frustrated leaders, disenfranchised outsiders, and organizations mired in a broken culture. Even firms with positive cultures can hire so many outsiders that the culture is overwhelmed by different and often conflicting aspirations, norms and communication styles. This inevitably leads to turmoil and leadership actions that are inconsistent with the cultural norms of the organization.

Assimilating outside talent – particularly at higher levels – is challenging. It must take into account the chemistry of the entire leadership team and the culture of the organization and use these tipping points to their strategic advantage.

Conclusion

Every organization has a culture. Make sure that you mix the right ingredients, and have the right chemistry to create a culture cake that reflects your firm's long-term vision. Then enjoy your just desserts.

Innovative Brand Building for a New Marketplace

Michael A. Donahue
Partner, LYFE Kitchen

Bio

Mike Donahue is a passionate brand storyteller. His unique combination of experience in sales, lobbying, public relations, government relations, public affairs and marketing yields an unconventional, yet multi-dimensional approach to brand building. He's worked for two of America's largest, well-known companies, as well as start-ups, public officials and celebrities. His obsession is helping to develop relevant, transformational cultures in existing or new brands to support the model of compassionate capitalism. Learning from the consumers who drive the marketplace, he's especially proud of developing the first Social Responsibility function at McDonald's, where he also served as Chief Communications Officer. He is the Co-Founder & Chief Brand Officer of LYFE Kitchen Restaurants, heralded as the "future of food" by *Wired* magazine, because of its chef inspired, great tasting menu that's also good for you, with a revolutionary socially responsible brand platform. He also advises other companies and clients on innovative brand building initiatives.

Key Points:

- The Brand Manager's Dilemma – We're Sales Reps Too.
- Innovate – Blue Ocean Theory.
- This is not your father's marketplace. Know Your Customer.
- Be a Leader, Not a Victim.
- Build and Protect Your Brand with an AIM Mentality.

The branding landscape: *future shock* has arrived.

Branding has become as provocative as religion and politics. There are as many theories as there are fragmented channels of distribution. Market segmentation is as diverse, geographically and culturally, as any time in the history of the American Free Enterprise system.

"Big data" enables great brands to have all of the primary and secondary data they will ever need. But the strategies and messages still rely on the smarts and intuition of executives in charge. Start-up companies that don't focus on their "unique selling proposition (USP)" can quickly be viewed as irrelevant if they fail to cut through the noise and clutter barraging today's consumer.

In the 1970 book, *Future Shock*, Alvin Toffler predicted that companies and consumers would experience a biological and psychological reaction from too much change within a short time. He must have glimpsed the technological explosion of cable, smart phones, apps, and the speed and vastness of the Internet.

Today's CEO must rely on brand, marketing and communication staff as their customer relevancy barometer, or run the risk of having their "brand trees fall in a forest and make no sound".

The brand manager's dilemma.

I'll never forget the time as an up-and-coming media relations executive that I anxiously approached a member of top management with a potentially brand threatening crisis. I walked in his office and was greeted with, "You Media Relations people…you're like going to the dentist, a necessary evil." After providing the obligatory "courtesy chuckle" I delivered the root canal of a dilemma, and for the next 72 hours all hands were in a war room, doing all we could to mitigate the damage of this unplanned, unscheduled, and unbudgeted management inconvenience.

CEOs have to rethink their view of Communications, PR and Branding. In this media-frenzied world, the damage that can be done to a brand is instantaneous—and a rapid, strategic response is as critical to the future of the business as the response to a product failure or class action suit. Yet, some brand pros will tell you that they are viewed as non-critical functions when compared to other departments.

The fact is that CEOs are under such pressure for results in their ever-shrinking lifespan, that the calendar diverts them from what's really going on with the preferences of the multi-cultural quilt of customers in America today.

Innovate—blue ocean theory.

W. Chan Kim and Renee Mauborgne's 2005 international bestseller, *Blue Ocean Strategy: How to Create Uncontested Market Space and Make the Competition Irrelevant,* is required reading for every senior leader. Steve Jobs had the idea long before the book was published as he created breakthrough products that none of us knew we needed but now can't live without. He innovated. He blew up the box. He was a brand genius with his intuitive consumer focused decisions that revolutionized the world.

The bottom line: stop the benchmarking. The very act makes you look just like the others. Fortune 50 companies continue to fight over market share as profit pools dry up. Dare to be different. Obsess about understanding consumer trends and lifestyle needs. Come up with radical new ideas that will resonate with your target customers you have designed your products to serve.

Know your customer.

Learn from the mistakes of legions of companies that refused to listen, or react in a timely way to customers, competition or market factors. Think the tobacco industry, K-Mart and many others. Senior leaders and their employees may no longer represent the diversity of their customers and may miss the mark as a result.

Customers are usually ahead of the market. Successful entrepreneurs mine those consumer insights, discover the need, innovate, and solve problems or create a new product or service. Here is an adage for the times: "The big no longer eat the small, the fast eat the slow". If you study *Red Bull's* success in the energy drink category, you understand how slow the beverage giants were to respond.

Toffler was right. The rate of change is making mega, savvy brands look stuck in quick sand, and too many have sunk. Beware of those professing the answer is a new fad, trend, website, or app. So many brand "experts" repeat the latest absolutes they read in a magazine, blog, or post. Listen carefully if you hear "it's all about" something because you'll realize that one day it's "all about health", the next "millennials", and next week the newest buzz word or best seller.

Bottom line, when it comes to attracting customers, it's never about just one thing. No "sound bite" management please: that's how brands lose credibility, trust and relationships with formerly loyal customers. Know what you know, and more importantly what your limitations are, as you build your team.

Be obsessive, read everything you can, test/taste/feel products in the design phase with real customers. Be a sponge not a fountain. Listen to consumers. Use primary and secondary research and find experts who can save you time, money and resources to avoid going down rabbit holes.

Be a leader, not a victim.

Private industry used to scorn bureaucracy, ridicule inefficiencies of government, and moan about lack of leadership from elected officials. They held the high ground because their companies were efficient, expeditious, honest, and profitable. Today bureaucracy and inefficiency have permeated companies and they have lost the courageous leadership that ignited innovation.

Slick advertising campaigns, slogans, and 30 or 60 second commercials no longer resonate with customers. Transparency and authenticity are no longer words that define brand essence. The quote "who you are speaks so loudly, I cannot hear what you say" describes consumer purchasing patterns. They measure with all five senses and more frequently a "sixth sense"–social consciousness about how you operate. The most important element of every relationship is trust, and American customers are increasingly cynical towards those who are not grounded in socially responsible policies and procedures.

If you are in the restaurant industry, make bold decisions and tell your story. Make no compromises when it comes to "operating in good taste, rather than just simply tasting good". Support sustainable building and sourcing. It might cost a bit more, but you will be rewarded by customers who vote with their feet on those brands they feel care about most about their values and beliefs.

Operate in an anticipatory issues management mentality: AIM.

You might notice that I like smart quotes from smart people. JFK had yet another one, not as famous as some, when he said, "the best time to fix the roof is when the sun is shining." An oil filter company used to advertise "pay me now…for preventative maintenance or pay me later, when we rebuild your engine".

Too many companies focus on expense control, not revenue growth. They make shortsighted decisions that end up costing the brand and/or shareholders dearly in market value and brand equity. Sometimes this means they choose crisis management over anticipatory leadership and don't have contingency funds set aside for what are predictable events.

An oil spill, foreign bodies in food products, product defects or other unfortunate incidents aren't a "crisis". They can be anticipated and forecasted by pioneering leaders who make AIM a priority. It's simply good business. And, it's much more effective than scrambling to train an otherwise composed executive to face the bright lights of the media. Contingency plans, messaging and influential allies can all be organized in advance.

The concept of AIM was codified by a brilliant Ph.D. at Proctor & Gamble who saw it as a way to collaborate with routine adversaries to make informed or mediated decisions that replace critical or negative brand campaigns with advance problem solving.

The day should come when CEOs can ban the concept of "crisis management" because they have built a culture and brand protection unit that mitigates risk or avoids it all together. Creating a unit dedicated to the easily found concepts of AIM will go a long way to ensure that your company is a leader, not a victim.

Getting the
Cross Border Deal Done

David Spitulnik
Partner, Altura Group

Bio

David Spitulnik has been a successful executive with large, multinational companies and a strategy consultant to leaders of mid-market and closely held businesses. He develops and implements strategies that drive transformation, growth, diversification, and value creation. He has broad governance experience on not-for-profit, corporate and advisory boards in the US, Israel, Chile, Russia and Azerbaijan. David earned his BA from Haverford College and his MBA from Northwestern University's Kellogg School of Management. David and his wife, Diana, live in Evanston, IL.

Key Points

- When leading deals, it is critical to control the flow of information to the other side, from those below *and* above you in your organization.
- When forming international partnerships, the key is to understand the culture of your company and your partner's, and also the culture of the country in which you will be operating.
- When you return to a country after an extended absence, revisit the current cultural norms that govern doing business.

The Deal

Fifteen days after I joined Motorola in the newly formed Joint Ventures team, I was in a conference room in Madrid with executives from Telefonica discussing a venture to manufacture cellular systems equipment in Spain. Motorola had closed similar transactions in other divisions, but this was the first for the Cellular Infrastructure Division (CID). We recognized that to win the business away from a long time Telefonica supplier, Motorola had to commit to manufacture network elements with one of Telefonica's subsidiaries in Spain.

Before leaving for Madrid, the team met with the head of the Infrastructure Division to discuss our bargaining parameters and agree upon a course of action. We then negotiated over the next several months, edging closer to the boundaries regarding ownership, management and manufacturing commitments. Finally we hit a final barrier, could give no more, and flew home.

When I returned to the US, my first stop was to the office of the head of CID. I learned that while I was in transit from Spain, he had received a call from his counterpart in Madrid and had agreed to give more on one of the issues. Over the next two months, he would extend the boundaries two more times communicating directly with his counterpart without notifying me or the negotiating team.

Takeaway: When leading deals, it is critical to control the flow of information to the other side, from those below and above you in your organization.

Negotiations moved forward again and after a series of strenuous debates, we agreed that Motorola would be the majority owner and would lead the venture. Only one major issue remained: the official language of the venture.

Since this manufacturing partnership depended upon Motorola technology and Motorola's experienced US manufacturing teams, we took the position that the official language should be English. Since the venture was located in Spain and most employees would be Spanish, our counterparts took the position that the official language should be Spanish.

After several weeks of discussion, we agreed that English would be the official language. Except for a few minor details, we were ready to close the deal.

We scheduled a meeting at noon the following day to wrap up the details. Our team arrived at noon, but waited almost two hours for our counterparts. We were finally brought into the conference room, and when our host asked what we wanted to do about lunch, I suggested that since we were two hours behind schedule, we should bring lunch in. Our host looked at me and said, "David, lunch is as important to the Spanish as English is to Motorola."

On the way to lunch, my counterpart linked arms with me. The rest of my team was a bit ahead, but looked back and wondered at the sight of two men walking arm in arm down the street. Over the course of that four block walk, we talked about and resolved the remaining issues. When we were seated at the restaurant, I told my team that we could celebrate the deal being done, and that all that was left to do was to memorialize the agreement. We also celebrated the fact that we had successfully resolved internal issues as well as those with our new partner.

Over the next several years, Motorola provided tens of millions of dollars of products and services to Telefonica under this contract. We had learned how to listen, to be open to other approaches, and created an agreement that recognized the strengths of two great industry leaders and two countries.

Conclusions

When forming international partnerships, it is important to understand the culture of your respective companies, and the cultural norms of the country in which you will be operating.

When I left Motorola after 17 years, my sons asked me how many countries I had traveled to on behalf of the company. It turned out that the number was 75. In several cases, I did a deal, left and went back many years later to do another. It was refreshing to revisit the original deal partners as well as my original impressions of the country and its culture. In most, if not all cases, the culture had shifted making it necessary to again relearn the basics of doing a transaction with people from another culture.

When you return to a country after having been gone for a while, take time to relearn cultural norms that govern doing business.

Suggested Reading

"The Top Ten Ways That Culture Can Affect International Negotiations" – Ivey Business Journal, http://iveybusinessjournal. com/topics/global-business/the-top-ten-ways-that-culture-can-affect-international-negotiations#.VCiUnCldVOh

Networking: The Key to Launching a Successful Business

Steve Morris

CEO, Asset Strategies Group

Bio

Steve Morris is the Founder and CEO of Asset Strategies Group, LLC. Since founding ASG, he has worked with over 80 specialty retailers, offering business services and solutions focused entirely on the specialty store real estate supply chain. Prior to founding ASG, Steve was CFO and CAO of Limited Brand's Real Estate and Store Design and Construction shared service organization and responsible for a $1 billion annual occupancy expense budget and over $300 million in annual capital spending. A Harvard MBA, he has more than 25 years' experience working in department store, big box and specialty store retail organizations.

Key Points

- Successful networking is how I started my business and is our key to success.
- Networking provides sales leads and sometimes, unexpected, invaluable advice.
- Networking isn't about *you*. It is about how you can help each other.
- Networking can be defined as building relationships that will enrich your life.

What You Need to Know

I've worked in multiple industries, in big companies and small, in times of growth and restructuring, and I pretty much enjoyed it all. So my life experiences did not provide much of a guidepost when I landed on the Shields Meneley "couch", with the big "What's next?" sign on my forehead.

I had learned that big companies and small have their own dynamics and drama, but the next big "corporate" gig was going to be delayed for family health reasons. We were anchored in Columbus, Ohio, and at age 55, the clock was ticking. I was not poor, but neither did I have the resources to bankroll an early retirement or finance a business. So I did what many do—hung up my "consultant" shingle to stay even financially and think about what was next.

Then 9/11 happened, and the job market evaporated. A friend was developing the concept of store-branded Visa cards, so I offered to help him network with retailers. I pitched the idea to another friend who was the CFO at a Columbus retailer. He was lukewarm about the idea. But during that conversation, he lamented not having services that my group had brought to the Limited Brands Real Estate Department. He asked why I didn't put together a little company to provide those services.

When I was the CFO and CAO of Real Estate and Store Development at Limited Brands, it owned 12 businesses. As an aside, real estate occupancy costs are the biggest expense for specialty retailers, and store construction and lease obligations consume the most capital by far. I was hired to "fix things" and had spectacular success, reducing occupancy costs nearly 150 basis points in a little over three years, and creating lasting business processes and systems.

So, I knew how to do it, but feared I lacked the hard-driving, extroverted personality that I associate with successful entrepreneurs. The idea of starting a business at age 55, with limited capital, in the middle of a recession, was a non-starter. But, when I met with the CFO again a month later, he asked, "Why not?"

So I did what I was taught—I networked. I traveled to San Francisco to meet with Gap, ostensibly on a consulting proposition. But while I was there, I asked if I started this company doing XYZ, would they give us a contract? I did the same with Footlocker in New York, as well as Abercrombie and Justice. One great thing about specialty retail is that it's both a large industry and a small world. Forget seven degrees of separation. Think two degrees. So I was off and running with four promised contracts, and a best friend who worked for me at Limited who joined as a Partner in the start-up. We were cash positive from the beginning, and have bootstrapped our way to $5 million in annual revenue.

I've survived launching a company following the 9/11 recession, the worldwide meltdown, and the loss of a customer that represented 30% of our business (when they brought our work and most of our staff in-house!) My business partner, a critical asset to the business, left to pursue his dream of becoming a writer. And I can proudly state that in 12 years, we have worked with over 80 retailers on some aspect of their real estate, have between 20 and 25 active customers, with 80% revenue carry over from year to year.

We incorporate industry best practices, have great market knowledge, and strong leadership within the company. But these are the things that *allow* us to be successful, they don't *make* us successful.

This is what I believe: Successful networking enabled me to launch our business and is the key to our continued success. We have resisted hiring professional sales people because up to now, 100% of our opportunities have come from networking and referrals. We may need to rethink this at the next stage of growth, but it is the relationships that we have established and nurtured that got us here.

Networking is now a way of life for me. It not only generates sales leads, but it can also provide unexpected insights and invaluable advice. It connected me with our financial advisor, our accounting firm, and our marketing firm.

I also believe that networking is a two-way street. I've helped at least four real estate executives find their current positions and introduced other retail service entrepreneurs to retailers. This has resulted in sales or consulting assignments for them, and we are more than happy to meet over coffee or lunch to share leads and ideas.

Columbus is a great mid-market city. We may have the highest per capita population of retail executives in the country, and we're strong on restaurant and distribution talent, too. Some days I seem to be the first stop when someone has left a company and is looking for their "next". And I am genuinely happy to talk, and occasionally able to add contacts to their network. At age 66, I am always looking for new people to meet with fresh, interesting ideas and perspectives.

Conclusion

Networking was critical to launching our successful business and building our customer base. But, business growth isn't linear. Growing pains might be a "nice problem to have" but size will bring new organizational challenges. I need to talk to people who have grown businesses from $5 million to $15 million so that we can anticipate and plan for this next stage of growth, so I am networking on how to establish an advisory board. Beyond that, I am looking to connect with engaged, energized business leaders who maintain their edge into their 70s. There will be more of us each year who choose to work into their late 60s and 70s because we are healthy, active, and enthusiastic about the future. And for those of you who are decades younger, remember: Our networks are *priceless*, and they took a lifetime to develop.

Paying It Forward

Peter Hong
Treasurer, Alcoa Inc.

Bio

Peter joined Alcoa Inc., a global leader in lightweight metals technology, engineering, and manufacturing, in April 2007 as vice president and treasurer. He served previously as the corporate treasurer for four other large multinational corporations, including Case Corporation and Ingersoll-Rand Company. Prior to serving as a corporate treasurer, Peter worked in corporate banking for First Chicago (a J.P. Morgan predecessor) and Citibank. Peter serves on the board of City Year New York. He is also actively involved with Northwestern University, serving on its Library Board of Governors, the New Jersey Alumni Admissions Council, and the New York Leadership Council.

Key Points

- Relentlessly leverage your technical knowledge and analytical skills.

- Never forget that the best interest of the shareholders is "True North."
- Maintain a nurturing environment.
- Constantly develop talent.
- Pay it forward.

Background

Mine is a classic immigrant story. My parents were unskilled laborers. They raised two sons in a blue collar Chicago neighborhood, both sons attended Chicago public schools, and both now hold advanced business degrees.

I received my BA in economics and an MBA in accounting and finance from Northwestern University in five years. I aspired to a Fortune 500 finance career, and spent my first thirteen years in corporate banking at two multinational banking firms. These assignments provided an outstanding foundation for a successful transition to the client side. I have now served as corporate treasurer for five Fortune 500 firms in diverse industries, including commodities, industrial manufacturing, and telecommunications.

My original career goals were: Fortune 500 corporate treasurer by year 15; a Fortune 500 CFO by year 20. These goals were rooted in the classic view that success in finance equated to reaching the CFO position. While the first goal was achieved, the second has been elusive because the real world also has an impact on even the best laid plans.

I have survived a number of mergers, made it through the changes in the executive suite, and found that each transition required me to prove myself again in the Treasurer's role. These changes also meant that I hadn't had the opportunity to gain the operational finance experience that has now become the "missing ingredient".

Early in my present – and fifth – tenure as a Fortune 125 Corporate Treasurer, I accepted that the window to achieving the goal of CFO was closing. At the same time, I realized that I was gaining enormous satisfaction from mentoring others and creating pathways for them to be confident, to make bold moves, and to be even more successful.

Their successes are also mine in my role as a finance professional, a corporate executive, a career coach, and, most importantly, a parent. I have learned that lateral growth is as gratifying and compelling as the ascent to the pinnacle where only one can dwell. And, I believe that I have become a better role model as a result.

What I've Learned

Relentlessly leverage your technical knowledge and analytical skills.

My business school concentrations were accounting and finance. I did not sit for a CPA or CFA certification, but made sure that I remained current on innovative financing techniques and accounting and regulatory changes. I took every opportunity to learn from my broad network of finance industry contacts, and learned to solve very complex business challenges. I understood how finance could drive profitable sales growth and how to structure joint-venture transactions with minimal direct investments. In each role at a "new" firm, this broad financial experience served me well.

The best interests of the shareholders are the "True North".

My guiding principle is always "do what is best for the shareholder". This mantra is a powerful consensus-building mechanism that overcomes hidden agendas that can be detrimental to the shareholder. It is an unassailable test to resolve opinion differences or avert suboptimal choices. My colleagues have told me how much they value this consistent focus since they can rely on my objectivity in any situation.

Constantly develop talent and maintain a nurturing environment.

"Human capital" is more than a catch phrase. A firm's success is its people. I focus intensely on talent development and employee engagement, and employee surveys demonstrate that we have sharply improved team morale and performance. Our unit is viewed as the spawning ground for emerging senior-level talent and individuals seek me out for growth opportunities. Assignments within the corporate treasury function – traditionally a "black box", non-core unit in most firms – became increasingly attractive.

"Pay it forward."

My parents gave me the only guidance they could. Study hard. In the less complicated world of yesterday, I succeeded by following their wise counsel.

The world is vastly different in today's information age, and the gap between the "haves" and "have nots" is growing. Those from more affluent families seem to have every opportunity, but those with limited access to guidance and technology are at a significant disadvantage. This lack of structure and support severely compromises one's ability to succeed no matter how bright or capable.

So now I am "paying it forward". I am an active mentor passing along simple, core lessons to an expanding group of individuals with vastly different means. This group includes young adults in New York housing projects, college graduates committing a year of service in New York grammar schools, and students at my alma mater. I help them understand their unique skills and experiences and articulate those differentiators to potential employers.

Conclusion

The intellectual and professional rewards from my professional role have been great but the psychic rewards for "paying it forward" have been profound and infinite. My personal definition of success now reflects not only my perceived or actual career accomplishments, but the deep understanding that my personal happiness has come from defining my contributions in a much broader way. May you find similar rewards.